James Hanna (signature)

Cornbread and Beans for Breakfast

The Misadventures of a Boy Growing Up In
The South During The Thirties And Forties

James Milton Hanna

Cornbread and Beans for Breakfast
Copyright 1994
By James Hanna

Library of Congress Catalog Card Number 94-70707

ISBN O-9640458-O-X

Fifth Printing, 2001

Other books by author:
A Possum in Every Pot
The Labrador Saga
Beyond Yonder Ridge
A Man Called Shiloh
Tales From Delaware Bay
Milton's Guide to Self-Publishing
Southern Tales (English / Spanish)

Cherokee Books
P.O. Box 463
Little Creek, DE 19961

Printed by
Quill Publications
Columbus, Georgia 31908

Table of Contents

Acknowledgments / Dedications

To my grandchildren who often asked for a Milton story before bedtime and to those who lived during the time depicted in Milton's stories.

To my wife and children who have heard the Milton stories many times and whose support has insured that the saga will survive the author.

To those who have gone on before, many prematurely. They are remembered with fondness.

To Nora Howell for her illustrations.

A special thanks to Thomas Amos, outstanding illustrator, for the cover.

Introduction
The Great Depression

Times were hard. The Great Depression had descended like a tornado. It was no longer a matter of escaping harm, but of survival itself. Those days were particularly bad because many adults had known better times—times when jobs were always available for those wishing to work. Now jobs were few; money was scarce. Many folks had lost all they owned, but their pride and self respect. They were deeply hurt because they had trusted a system that, they had been told, couldn't possibly fail. Yet it had. The great United States of America had, without warning, been brought to her knees.

It was during the Depression that Milton entered the world, a time that many of us look back to with pride, if for no other reason than we had survived it, and a yearning for the closeness between people that had been forged during those difficult times. Milton grew up in the small Alabama community of Valdosta, near Tuscumbia. Valdosta was a small village of, perhaps, 200 people. There were three stores, each located in a different section of the village. It was bisected by a main road with houses on both sides and four intersecting streets about one-half mile long, extending to Highway 72, which paralleled the railroad. Two churches—Baptist and Church of Christ— served the community.

Everyone knew everyone else in Valdosta, and a child would normally behave because neighbors would almost certainly report any wayward actions that had escaped the notice of parents. And punishment was sure to follow, either from the belt, razor strap, or (the greatest indignity of all) having to cut one's own switch from a peach or plum tree.

In time, Milton became very experienced in cutting his own switch. He had even learned to notch it in several places so that it would break into short pieces after a few lashes from his mother. Being a mother, however, Milton's mom soon learned what her son had been up to and began inspecting the switches herself. If she suspected tampering, Milton would have to cut another, or, worse, she would cut it herself—invariably a longer one—and give him an extra swat. Milton by and large accepted his punishment, perhaps realizing that his behavior justified it. Of course, this was before child-abuse was the concern it is today. In Milton's time. spanking was virtually synonymous with proper child-rearing and did, in fact, tend to get the attention of a "back-sliding" child.

If contemporary child-abuse laws had existed in Milton's time, it is quite likely that the entire adult population of Valdosta would have been "doing time." Indeed, the outline of a plum or peach switch seemed permanently imprinted on Milton's bare legs during much of his youth. Still, Milton figured, the whippin's kept him straighter than he would have been, and he sometimes wonders why today's "experts" are so quick to spare the rod.

In sum, the village of Valdosta was a fine place to spend one's youth; children bounded and abounded and the crime rate was all but non-existent. Most everyone had one thing in common—little or no money. In those day, few teens had cars. Television was still years away, and the only "weed" or "grass" folks knew about was what was hoed from the corn and cotton fields. Just about the worst thing a teen could do was drink a beer, and none dared do that openly.

Children had to be far more creative in their pursuit of entertainment and fun, relying more on friends, family, and the goodness of nature than today's indoor video-oriented kids. Milton often reflects on how simple his early life was compared with life-styles of today's teens. He yearns again for those days, a time of dear friends and gentle people, and wonders, as had his grandfather before him, why the younger generation has "gone to the dogs."

JMH

Chapter 1
Where It Started

The year was 1932. The time was 8:36 AM. The event was the birth of a baby boy in Cherokee, Alabama. And omens were present everywhere: sirens wailed, bugles blared, drums rolled, and a comet streaked across the morning sky. At least, that's the way Milton would have preferred it. In reality, his birth was as routine as any other, occurring in the back room of his parent's three-room house, with old Doc Whitlock supervising.

Sirens, however, did wail as the police chased a Model T past the house on Highway 72 toward Iuka, Mississippi. And the braying of a mule in the backyard might have been mistaken for a bugle, and most anyone would have mistaken the thundering of roller skates on the newly black-topped front street for a drum roll. As for the comet, well grandfather's slow-footed old sow did get "launched" by a passing wagon.

But, truth be told (something not always easy for Milton to own up to), his birth was as undramatic as any other in the Depression era of North Alabama. Of course, his father and mother were overjoyed: his father because he was so proud to have sired a son; and his mother, well, she was happy that the pain was finally over and that her son was "all there"; you know, ten fingers, ten toes, etc. When Doc Whit-

9

lock spanked him into life. Thereafter, it seemed to Milton, it was always being spanked out of him. Milton soon made it known that his lungs and his appetite were also in perfect working order.

Of course, Milton would have no memories of the event, blessed or otherwise. But among his earliest memories was the time his father sat him atop a fence post one starry night and pointed out the North Star and the Big Dipper. The stars seemed so big that he thought he might reach up and touch them. That was a moment he would remember the rest of his life.

His next memory was a bit more down to earth—his first spanking with a switch. It happened this way: an older boy told Milton's mother that he had been bird-hunting and had killed several birds that he had thrown away. The older boy had earlier given Milton a slingshot and taught him how to use it. The next day, slingshot in hand, Milton told his mother he was going bird-hunting. He walked up the fence row and returned in about ten minutes. When his mother asked him if he had any luck, he said he had killed three birds but had thrown them away.

The story sounded a bit too familiar to Milton's mom, but her son insisted he was telling the truth. He further said that two of the birds were black with red stripes and the other was green with red dots. Not about to let him off the hook, his mom asked Milton to show her where he had disposed of the birds.

So together they walked the fence row until Milton finally said he could not "remember" where he had thrown the birds. Once home, his mom again asked if he had really killed the birds of such unusual colors. When Milton held to his story, she lectured him on the evils of lying and followed the lecture with a lashing using a small peach limb. This, too, was a moment he would remember the rest of his life.

Chapter 2
Milton Discovers Skunks

Milton learned to read at an early age and developed a healthy interest in adventure and the great outdoors. His enthusiasm for nature came naturally enough, growing up in rural North Alabama and surrounded by kin who, when not hunting or fishing, were telling stories of their outdoor adventures. In particular, there was Uncle Addison who fished, hunted, and paid his way through school by trapping wild animals and selling their pelts. Milton spent many hours in the company of Uncle Addison, either stalking game or perched on a creek bank, listening to fascinating tales of his uncle's youth.

By the time he was ten, Milton was reading everything he could find on hunting, fishing, and trapping; he wanted to know it all. In those days, Sears, Roebuck and Co. purchased animal pelts, and Milton sent for a list of fur prices. Among the pelts that Sears bought were skunk pelts, offering a top price of $3.50 for the largest ones. Previously, the most Milton had earned was a dollar or two a day picking cotton in the punishing heat of the Alabama sun. That autumn, Milton began planning to become a great skunk trapper. Clearly, that's where the money was. And in North Alabama, skunks were everywhere—if not always seen, certainly scented. Indeed, he couldn't believe that such a pretty animal could have such a bad odor.

Milton didn't have a trap, but he did have a "trapper": his small but absolutely fearless "tree" dog, Jigs. One cold, fall day, Milton and Jigs were crossing a field when Jigs locked on to an animal scent, eventually tracing it to a pile of rocks that had been cleared from the field years earlier.

Small trees had grown up through the rocks, but there was still enough space between them were an animal might hide. Jigs began circling the rock pile, looking for a way into the tunnels within the pile.

By now, Milton had become as excited as Jigs and began moving the rocks to help Jigs do his job. As he picked up one of the rocks, he glimpsed the quick movement of an animal. He quickly removed more of the rocks, exposing a tunnel. Again the animal darted. He grabbed at it and caught the animal by the tail, pulling it struggling from the rocks.

The next few seconds did more to educate Milton than all the reading he had done in the past year. For he held before him a skunk that, from all indications, had seen better days. Before he could react, the skunk unloaded on him, spraying musk on his face, then over his entire body. When Milton let go of the tail, Jigs attacked the skunk, but managed only to make it angrier. The skunk fired a parting shot at both Jigs and Milton, and almost leisurely re-entered its den, proud of its success in battle.

If Milton had any lingering interest in skunks, it was buried beneath his desire to get home. And his mother knew he was coming well before he set foot in the door. She made him take off his clothes and bury them in the garden. She then scrubbed him with tomato juice in an attempt to neutralize the odor. But it still took two weeks for Milton to recover from his skunk encounter.

While recovering from the "great rock-pile incident", Milton still dreamed of being a trapper and living in the great outdoors. Despite his lesson in reality, he wanted to be a professional trapper more than ever. He could not get the idea of riches out of his mind.

Within a week of his recovery, he had received his traps from Sears. His grandmother gave him a can of cracklings (or pork skins, as they are known in the North) to use as bait. So it was again that he set out in his quest for skunk pelts, selecting a thick stand of pine trees to set his first trap. He built a pen, scattered a handful of pork crackling in the back, and concealed a steel trap under pine needles at the entrance to the pen.

After a sleepless night, Milton arose at the crack of dawn, got through his breakfast in record time, and hurried to the woods and his first trap. He could never remember being this excited as he trounced through the woods on yet another crisp November morning. Both his heart and his lungs were bursting with the goodness of life. He would be able to see the trap in just a few seconds.

He was not disappointed. Before him stood a large, solid black, and very angry skunk. The trap had closed on just a single toe. Milton's heart raced, for trapping a skunk was one thing, but the pelt of a black skunk was worth much more to Sears than the regular variety.

His excitement soon gave way to reality, however, for he had never considered how he might "dispatch" it. And the skunk seemed in no mood to be dispatched. He had read that trapped skunks were normally shot through the head to preserve the pelt. But, of course, young Milton didn't own a rifle. It was Jigs that would determine the outcome of the encounter.

The feisty dog confronted the skunk and, with the animal's attention diverted, Milton clubbed it over the head with a big stick. The blow, instead of knocking the skunk out, only knocked it out of the trap, and once again Milton and Jigs got it with "both barrels".

Milton and Jigs raced for home, while the skunk leisurely wandered off nursing a sore toe.

Milton suspecting that once he got there, he would have more to nurse than the skunk would. To his surprise, his mother didn't whip him, but she did threaten to disown him and send him to reform school if he ever again got sprayed by a skunk.

He went through the tomato-juice deodorizing process again and was sick for three weeks following his second encounter with a skunk. While recuperating, he spent his time reading about trapping and made plans for yet another trap line as soon as he was up and about. Needless to say, he said nothing of his plans to his mother, figuring—as any lad would—that she just wouldn't understand. And besides, he would be better prepared next time. After all, $3.50 for just one skunk pelt!

Chapter 3
Milton's First Camping Trip

When Milton was ten years old, he decided that he was going camping. He had heard older boys discussing their camping trips, so he decided that he, too, would become a camper. He talked to his grandfather and mother about camping. They asked him where he wanted to go camping and he told them that he would camp on the far edge of his grandfather's farm. They agreed to Milton's request, so he gathered an old quilt and his hatchet, told everyone goodbye, and walked the quarter of a mile to the woods.

It was a crisp, fall evening when Milton and his small, brown and white dog, Jigs, arrived at the edge of the woods. Since darkness was setting in, Milton decided to camp under an oak tree that had a nice spread of lower limbs. He raked up a pile of leaves for a bed and spread his quilt over them. He and the dog lay down and covered themselves with the quilt. Everything was comfortable and Milton lay there petting his dog and listening to the night sounds. He could hear cattle mooing in the distance and an occasional dog barking. The evening sounds contributed to a feeling of loneliness and he felt like returning home. He was too proud not to finish what he had started, so he remained where he was and drifted off to sleep.

Sometime later in the night, Milton's dog suddenly

jumped up from their quilt bed and started growling. Milton, his heart beating fast, sat up with his arm around his pet listening for what had alerted him. At first, he couldn't hear anything, but then he heard it. SOMETHING was approaching from deep within the woods. He could hear something walking through thick leaves. The leaves were dry and crunchy. The approaching creature was treading heavily and the leaves and twigs were snapping as it neared.

Jigs began growling louder with deep rumblings from his chest, and the hair stood up on his back. Jigs backed up against Milton as far as he could. The sound came nearer and Milton leaped from his bed for the lower limbs of the oak tree

He rapidly climbed fifteen feet up the tree. He wondered if the creature could climb? What if the noise was from a bear or a lion? Then, thankfully, he remembered that there were no bears or lions in Alabama.

The dog went crazy and charged into the night. He chased a cow into the open past Milton's tree. The cow let out a loud moo and fled across the field with the dog in hot pursuit. Soon the dog returned and lay down on Milton's quilt and was soon fast asleep. Milton decided to sleep the remainder of the night up in the tree. His heart was still beating fast and he was too shaky to climb down from the tree, even if he had wished to.

Milton got little sleep on the limbs up in the oak tree. He would doze off on occasion. He had never realized before the many sounds that come from the woodland at night. He was awakened by an owl hooting from a nearby tree. Later, Milton heard foxes barking from the mountain ridges, and he heard a loud screech from some animal being caught. He had never dreamed that so much was occurring at night in the woods. A number of times his dog would start growling, but he never left the base of the tree.

Milton was awakened by a rooster crowing, and he could see lights being lit in homes nearby. Soon he could hear doors slamming, dogs barking, and cattle mooing. As the sun arose over the horizon, Milton and his dog returned home to a good breakfast. The dog ate and then vanished for two days. Jigs was finally found at the base of the oak tree where Milton had camped. He was guarding the old quilt that Milton had neglected to take home with him.

Milton's night in the woods had been very educational and was the first of many camping trips that would take him to various areas of North Alabama.

Chapter 4
The Christmas Gift

As Christmas of 1942 approached, Milton found it difficult to get into the spirit of things. After all, America was at war—a difficult thing for anyone to grasp, let alone a ten-year-old boy whose father had recently died- He had been killed in 1939 in Mt. Pleasant, Tennessee. And to make matters worse, Milton wanted something for Christmas that he knew he couldn't possibly get: a Red Ryder air rifle. In his heart, he knew he was dreaming: a gift as precious as an air rifle was well beyond his mother's ability to provide. She worked in a jewelry store and made $18.50 a week. And every cent of that went for food and a minimum of clothing. Milton did receive a new pair of shoes each fall in time for school, along with three pairs of overalls and three shirts. His winter coats were those outgrown by older relatives and friends. It wasn't that he was ungrateful—indeed, he was thankful for everything he had. Still, he very much wanted that BB gun.

Most of the boys in Valdosta already knew what they were getting for Christmas—a Red Ryder BB gun. The year before, most of the ten-year-old boys had received air rifles; those who had turned ten in the past year figured it was their turn this Christmas. One of the boys had even learned that he would be getting a pony and a saddle, since he had received an air rifle last Christmas. Needless to say, he was one very happy lad and envied by every boy in Valdosta. In a game of cowboys and Indians, he would have everything but the indians. The rest of the boys either rode mules in their play or, more frequently, ran.

When Milton's friends asked him what he was getting for Christmas, he found himself saying that he didn't really need anything because he had received so many presents last Christmas. But, oh, he really wanted that Red Ryder BB gun more than he had ever wanted anything in his young life. He expected that he would get some chocolate drops and a few apples and oranges. His mother always provided as well as she could for both Milton and his younger sister. He hoped that his sister would get a doll for Christmas, for she wanted a doll every bit as much as Milton wanted the air rifle.

Christmas Eve finally arrived. Milton's mother had to work late at the jewelry store and stayed even longer for an employees' appreciation party. So Milton and his sister went to bed. While he couldn't quite suppress the excitement of Christmas, he was still sad that he wouldn't be getting the one

thing that he wanted most in life. So he tossed and turned all night, alternating between excitement and disappointment.

Milton's sister, Freida, finally awakened him at 5 AM, and they went to peek at what was under the tree. Milton didn't expect much for himself, but he did hope that his sister wouldn't be too disappointed.

She would not be: a large doll had been propped up so that it was sitting under the tree. The doll was wearing a beautiful red dress with white high-heel shoes. His sister was as happy as a puppy, and Milton was happy for her. Also under the tree for them were large socks packed with apples, oranges, nuts, and candy. Just as Milton was about to return to bed, he noticed a long box wrapped in green paper on the other side of the tree.

The excitement was too much for him to bear. He ran to the tree and, with trembling hands, ripped the paper from the box. There before him was a gleaming Red Ryder air rifle and five tubes of copper-coated BBs. Milton's yell could be heard throughout the house, and quite probably beyond it. It was certainly enough to awaken both his mother and his grandparents; but merely seeing the joy that Milton radiated was worth any inconvenience they may have felt at being awakened early. For this had truly been the happiest Christmas that Milton and his little rosy-cheeked sister ever had.

She cherished her doll for years to come, and Milton—well, he was quite certain that his Red Ryder air rifle was the greatest gift anyone could ever receive. But perhaps it was Milton's mother who had received the greatest gift, for she had made her children happy beyond words.

Chapter 5
Church

From an early age, Milton went to church and Sunday School with his mother and grandfather. As for most young boys, church had little real meaning for him. This did not mean he was un-Christian; only that he was too young to understand. But he did understand many of the lessons of Sunday School, including the teachings of Jesus and that it was wrong to steal or to lie. He was taught that if he lived a good life, he would go to Heaven when he died. But, for the most part, these were just words to Milton, who did not lie or steal. Well, he didn't lie much, and he certainly never stole.

As Milton grew older, attending church became something of a social obligation and, often, more fun than he had expected. He and his friends would sit in a back pew and not rely entirely on the preacher for entertainment. Among their favorite forms of diversion was "goosing," whereby the tickled boy would have to yell out what was on his mind at that instant. More than once, Milton was responsible for directing the hostile stares of the congregation toward a friend, whom Milton had caused to yell out words rarely heard in church.

On occasion, frequently in the spring or summer, there would be a visiting minister who would hold a series of services during week nights. Of course, this was during the pre-air conditioning era, and the heat was usually oppressive. One such traveling evangelist with a very loud voice was soon on to the games of Milton and his friends, so Milton decided on a special treatment for the good gentleman. The idea he would later regret, but boys, after all, will be boys.

Milton spent that entire day looking for wasp nests, capturing the wasps, and placing them in a fruit jar. That evening, after the service had begun and the visiting minister was sitting beneath the open window in the front of the church, a hand reached over the window sill and dropped an open quart-jar of angry wasps next to the minister's chair. Milton did not linger. He had hoped that the wasps would sting the minister's bald head. He would later learn that the wasps caused a near-panic among the congregation. He successfully resisted any temptation to confess, perhaps because of the whippings that would be sure to follow—several peach limbs worth to be sure.

Milton's cousin Charles was involved in the national Golden Gloves boxing program. After all, Joe Lewis, Heavyweight Champion of the World, was from Alabama, so it was only natural that local interest in boxing would be high.

Milton would have been interested, too, if he had not disliked being hit. Charles was a year older than Milton, and the cousins spent much time together. One night after church, the boys were horsing around at the back of the church. Charles kept "practicing" on Milton, poking him lightly despite Milton's continued objections. Frustrated with his role as a punching bag, Milton suddenly hit Charles in the face as hard as he could. Fortunately for Milton, the other boys in the area grabbed Charles before he could retaliate. Eventually Charles forgot the incident, and the cousins remained good friends.

As Milton grew older, the little Baptist Church in Valdosta became a more meaningful part of his life. It was in this church that Milton became a Christian. It happened this way.

A visiting minister was conducting a series of special services. The pastor was nice; he didn't yell at the boys as so many others had, and he could sing. Milton and several of his friends were sitting in a front pew, not because they wanted to but because they arrived late. The early birds usually got the back pews. The minister was preaching about the need to open one's heart to Jesus. To Milton, the minister seemed somehow to be speaking only to him. When the minister asked if anyone wanted Jesus to come into their heart, Milton was one of the first to step forward and accept Christ as his

Savior. Later that month, a special baptism service was held in a backwater slough on Bear Creek. It was a day service, which meant there would be no snakes. The water was muddy and cold, but the discomfort was no match for the spiritual comfort of baptism.

Milton will always remember that little Baptist Church in Valdosta with great fondness. He also remembers the goodness of the Sunday School teachers, who refused to grow discouraged in their attempts to reach teenagers (hardly the best audience) with the message of spiritual strength that the coming years would demand of them.

Chapter 6
Grandpa's Calf

When Milton was about ten, his grandfather took a large white-faced bull calf from the pasture and staked it in the yard to keep the grass down. This saved Milton from doing the mowing, but at noon each day, it was his responsibility to take the calf to water at Lily Pond, about a quarter-mile away.

Now, as farm chores go, this one was not particularly difficult. But the problem was that when it came time for watering, the calf grew playful. Not that Milton was anti-social, but have you ever had a seven-hundred pound play-mate? Milton was giving away about 620 pounds, so his reluctance was understandable.

The calf's favorite game was to charge Milton and to stop just short of hitting him, in the process half scaring him to death.

Milton would lead the bull calf by chain to the pond, never taking his eyes of the frisky calf for more than a few seconds. In the hand not holding the chain, Milton carried a big stick. When the bull would charge, as he eventually would, Milton would swing the stick. He usually missed, but on occasion he would have the satisfaction of landing a good blow. The bull didn't seem to mind, hit or miss.

Though Milton often complained to his grandfather

about the hazards of his job, his grandfather figured Milton was just trying to get out of the chore, trying to avoid going out into the hot noonday sun. After all, his grandfather would say, it was only a calf.

The situation finally became unendurable—and literally so—when the calf began poking Milton in the stomach with its broad head and lifting the boy off the ground. Fortunately for Milton, his small waist fit between the bull's six-inch horns. The bull calf would lift Milton into the air, shake him, and then toss him a few feet. When especially playful, the calf would even toss Milton over its head or shove him into the ground once it had him off his feet. It was no wonder that Milton lived in mortal terror of watering the calf.

Though the boy continued to complain to his grandfather, the chore remained his until the day Milton was running a temperature and was excused from his regular farm chores. His grandfather said that this time he would take the calf to Lily Pond for watering. Despite his temperature, Milton felt much improved.

Soon, Milton became aware that it was taking grandfather longer to water the calf than it took him. When his grandfather did return, his overalls were dirty, and the calf was not with him! His grandfather told Milton how sorry he was that he had not believed his grandson's horror stories about the bull calf. He told Milton that, on the way to the pond, the calf charged him and knocked him to the ground: he had to grab the bull's horns to prevent being gored. He said he wrestled with the calf for a long time and was able to prevent being injured only by beating the calf with its chain. He was finally able to force it into the pasture with the other cattle.

Milton's grandfather said the entire herd had gathered at the fence to watch the contest, just like people in the stands at a ballgame. A week later, the family was treated to some delicious steak and beef roasts, courtesy of a seven-hundred pound bull calf who would never again have the opportunity to make Milton's life miserable.

Chapter 7
The Smokehouse Incident

Each year, Milton's grandfather, a farmer, would slaughter several hogs, salt the meat, and store it in the smokehouse. The meat was meant to last the family the entire year. Bacon and fatback were stored in the wooden bins between layers of salt; bacon, hams, and shoulders were hung from the rafters after being treated with the preservative "Sugarcure." To this day Milton remembers the unique smell of the smokehouse: not an unpleasant odor but the musty scent that one associates with hickory-cured meat. It was Milton's job to retrieve meat from the smokehouse about once a week.

The smokehouse was just a darkened room attached to the barn; The trip to the smokehouse was not one Milton especially looked forward to because the only light in the room came from the opened door, and that light cast spooky shadows in the corners of the house. To make matters worse, rats had dug several small holes along the floor at the edge of the wall.

Once, when Milton was sent to the smokehouse for meat, he noticed in the dim light movement at one of the rat holes. But the movement was caused by no rat; rather, what he saw was a large, brightly colored snake, at least four-feet long, descending into one of the rat holes. Suddenly the bacon that his grandfather had sent him for was of no importance. He screamed and ran for the house. His grandfather, who heard Milton scream, met him and asked what had happened. Milton, in his excitement, blurted out that the smokehouse had been taken over by "a large snake, about ten-feet long!" He asked his grandfather to kill the snake, Milton firmly believing that the only good snake is a dead snake.

His grandfather replied that the snake had lived in the smokehouse for years and was not only harmless but actually beneficial because it ate only rats, mice, and other snakes. "Now go back and get the bacon that your grandmother wanted," he concluded. Milton knew that the request was not negotiable; his grandfather would tolerate no sass from his grandchildren.

So Milton returned to the smokehouse, apprehensively, and armed with a hoe. He cracked the door open just enough so that he could peer in.

He didn't see the snake so, ever so cautiously, he stepped into the smokehouse, allowing time for his eyes to adjust to the darkness. He tentatively reached for the slab of bacon, and there, coiled under the meat box, was the snake.

Milton felt his heart skip a beat. His first impulse was to take the hoe and convert this slithery nemesis into a "good snake." But, remembering his grandfathers admonition, he, instead, pressed the hoe against the coiled snake, hoping to keep it from striking him. But as soon the snake felt the hoe, it squirmed away from it, in the process striking at—but missing—Milton. That was enough for Milton. He raced through the door, leaving, snake, hoe—and, yes, bacon—behind. He stopped a few feet from the smokehouse door and turned to see if the snake had followed him. It hadn't. He was in a true dilemma: afraid to again face the snake and afraid to face his

31

grandfather without the bacon.

He summoned all the courage that he could and again peered through the smokehouse door. Waiting for his eyes to refocus to the darkness seemed like an eternity. Things appeared to be going his way: the snake was crawling into a rat hole. The snake was so wide that it appeared to be struggling to get through the hole. Milton found himself wishing that the snake would get struck and that the rats would eat it. Eventually, however, he saw the snake's tail disappear down the hole. Unable to take his eyes from the rat hole, Milton tiptoed into the smokehouse, ready to make his escape if the snake reappeared. His luck was holding. He grabbed the slab of bacon and made it out the door. He told his grandfather about the snake's striking out at him, but his grandfather refused to believe him.

Needless to say, Milton lived in dread the rest of the summer each time he would have to go to the smokehouse. While the snake seemed to have lost its fear of Milton, Milton's fear of the snake had grown, and he never entered the dark house without his trusty garden hoe. On each visit to the smokehouse (though he had begun to think of it in his mind as the "snake house"), the snake would coil and strike at Milton's shoes. But Milton used the hoe and his quickness of foot to avert the danger. He reported each encounter to his grandfather, but he assumed Milton was exaggerating in an attempt to get out of the smokehouse chore.

Then one day, when Milton was visiting one of his cousins, his grandfather went to the smokehouse for a ham. Without allowing time for his eyes to adjust to the darkness, he walked to the back of the room to fetch the ham from a hook. He suddenly felt something hit his heavy work shoe. He looked down just in time to see the big king snake coiling for another strike. He lost his balance, dropped the ham, and fell to his knees. He found himself eye to eye with the angry and hissing snake. He rolled quickly toward the door, the snake striking but hitting only the cloth of his grandfather's overalls.

He fled from the smokehouse, quite an accomplishment in itself because Milton's grandfather was a large and heavy man. When the motivation is strong enough, it's surprising the things ordinary folk can do. Once outside, grandfather seized the hoe, which was leaning against the smokehouse, and chopped the snake into "snake heaven," thereby making it one of Milton's "good snakes."

When Milton returned from his visit, his grandfather told him about his encounter with the snake. Taking the hoe with them to the smokehouse, in the event the "good snake" had some still-nasty relatives, Milton and his grandfather patched the rat holes so that snakes could never again enter the smokehouse. But the ghost of that snake must have lived on, because Milton could never again enter the smokehouse without first assuring himself that there was nothing slithering, coiling, or crawling in the many cracks and crannies of that old smokehouse.

Chapter 8
Snake Hunting

It was a warm spring day, altogether a wonderful day for Milton, 12, and his cousin Charles, 13, because school was over for the summer. Milton and Charles were spending the day hunting snakes or, for that matter, any wild creature that moved. They were armed with crude bows and arrows: the bows they had bent from red cedar limbs; the arrows they had made from firm weeds. The arrows were tipped with twenty-penny nails with their heads sawed off.

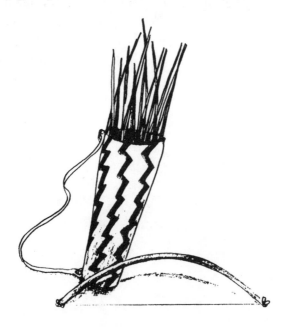

On previous hunting trips they had used real Indian arrowheads made from flint they had found along the Tennessee River. However, the flint heads were scarce and would often shatter when shot into white pine. Milton and Charles figured the Indians would have used twenty-penny nails, too, if they had the benefit of hardware stores.

Being a year older than Milton, Charles naturally assumed command of the expedition. Charles had red hair and a temper to match; to the best of Milton's knowledge, there was nothing that Charles was afraid of.

The boys decided they would try their luck at Dry Creek, which was not called "dry" for nothing. The "creek" was nothing more than a dry stream bed where water flowed only after a rainy period or sometimes during the winter. For the most part, however, the bed was quite dry with only an occasional pot hole of water to uphold its name. The "creek" was more of a rocky ravine, with many forms of stone and gravel littering the bed and slopes of the former stream. The banks of the dry bed consisted of a series of cracked and layered limestone formations—perfect places for snakes to dwell.

In North Alabama, the snakes most frequently encountered on a snake-hunt were racers, puff adders (hog-nosed snakes), an occasional copperhead or moccasin, and, rarer still, a rattlesnake. There were other snakes in the region, but these were nocturnal and not even the normally fearless Charles liked the combination of darkness and snakes. The boys pretended that nighttime snake-hunting was too impractical—it was just too hard to see snakes at night. But, in reality, the mere thought of it made their skin crawl.

As the two boys tramped over and around the rocks in the dry stream bed, their courage still largely intact, they heard a buzzing sound and instinctively jumped backwards. There, under a rock ledge just a few feet in front of them, a rattlesnake was coiled, its head up and its tongue flicking. The snake was probably no more than four-feet long, but to the cousins it might just as well have been a python. Later, when they told their parents of their run-in, they described the rattler as being between six and eight feet long. Their parents believed them because parents do not take lightly the dangers from poisonous reptiles when it is their children in harm's way.

Eventually, when they were able to recover their composure, the boys began shooting arrows at the snake. They scored several hits, and the gyrating, rattling snake crawled toward a crack in the cliff, looking like a mobile pin cushion with the many arrows sticking from its body. Indeed, the arrows protruding from its body prevented the rattler from slipping through the crack.

Because the boys began the day with only four arrows each, and had worked very hard to make them, they were not about to leave them with the snake, rattler or not. But, of course, the snake had other ideas. As they approached the rattler, it buzzed angrily and struck out at them. They tried to pull the arrows out using a long weed, but the snake would not cooperate. They looked for a large stick, but the rocky, dry stream bed was not the best place to find a tree limb. And the stones in the stream bed were either too small to be effective or too large to lift.

Charles, being the leader, decided to exercise his command and ordered Milton to retrieve the arrows. But Milton thought that the honor should go to Charles, the leader of the expedition. Eventually, agreeing that neither boy had a greedy bone in his body, they decided to let the rattler keep the arrows.

As the boys climbed the bank toward the road home, they began worrying that perhaps the rattler had angry relatives who were waiting to ambush them from the rocks along the bank. For that reason, it took the boys considerably longer to climb the bank than it had to walk down it. Of course, if one of the boys had snagged his pants on a piece of driftwood, they would have made the road -and their way home—in record time. In the years that followed, both Milton and Charles would maintain a healthy respect for snakes—especially tough rattlers.

Chapter 9
Milton Runs Away

Milton was not one to get into much trouble at home. It was not that he was such a good boy; it was more that he was seldom home. He spent nearly all of his spare time—after school, weekends, summer vacations—walking through the hills and along the streams.

He had two main chores to do each day: walking to the neighbor's well for water (his grandfather's home had no plumbing) and carrying the buckets home, and splitting wood then piling it beside the wood cook-stove.

Early one Saturday morning in late November, Milton went squirrel hunting. The evening before, he had taken only enough wood into the house to cook supper. He was going to bring the rest of the wood into the house before going hunting in the morning, but he had forgotten. When he returned home that afternoon, his grandfather was waiting for him and demanded to know why Milton had not brought all the · chopped wood into the house the previous evening.

It was Milton's main failing—and on this day, his undoing -that he was stubborn and had to have the last word. And his grandfather was, perhaps, the last man on the face of the Earth to have the last word with. Instead of offering an apology, Milton offered backtalk. His grandfather could not abide children being disrespectful to their elders. He told his grandson that he had gone too far and that he would have to teach Milton a lesson with his razor strap. Now Milton knew just how hard his grandfather could hit with a razor strap, and he also had come to feel that he was now too old to be beaten like a child.

So, as his grandfather approached with the strap, Milton took off. He hid under the house. But Jigs, Milton's dog, "snitched" on him by following him. His grandfather ordered him to come out and take his punishment, but Milton refused. His grandfather warned that Milton would have to come out sooner or later, and if it were later, the punishment would be harder. But Milton stayed put.

Eventually, when his grandfather had returned to the house, Milton decided to teach HIM a lesson: he would run away, and his grandfather would be forever sorry for the way he had treated his grandson. When he was certain his grandfather was no longer preoccupied with him, Milton crept out from under the house and made his way to the woodshed, where he kept his hatchet and camping equipment, including a backpack containing an old quilt and a skillet. He strapped on the backpack and hurried from the shed, being careful to keep the shed between himself and the house to keep his departure a secret.

Milton decided to make camp at the Government Reservation, a large tract along the Tennessee River comprising about two-thousand acres and two creeks that flowed into the river. It was a true wilderness area with acres of thick woods.

As he walked through the woods, Milton thought about how sorry his grandfather would feel and how much the rest of the family would miss him. He planned to remain at the Reservation for several years, living off the land just like the Indians of old.

For food, there were many nearby corn fields and an abundance of squirrels and rabbits, to say nothing of all the fish in the streams. He had also heard that wild goats lived on an island in the river. Though he had not thought to bring his rifle, he knew how to make a bow and arrows.

Before long, Milton envisioned himself eating goat meat and wearing their skins, much like Robinson Crusoe. Soon, meals of fried squirrel with baked apples or pears began to form in his mind. And just for the gathering, he could have all the walnuts, pecans, and hickory nuts he wanted. He remembered reading about Indians making bread from acorns, and it was hard to walk without tramping on an acorn. To Milton, his future as a fugitive from the strong arm of his grandfather began to look better each time he thought of it.

As evening approached, it soon occurred to Milton that his rifle was not the only important thing he had forgotten to bring. It was, after all, November, and his initial enthusiasm began to give way to the cold. He had forgotten to take a heavy coat. But Milton was, by now, no stranger to camping, and he knew a warm campfire would warm him body and soul—and he knew just the place.

Arriving at a grove of pine trees, Milton set up camp over a layer of pine needles several inches thick. He quickly constructed a lean-to shelter from several small trees, completing the job just before the sun slipped beneath the horizon. The temperature now was well below freezing, and Milton found that he could not banish thoughts of the warm wood stove at home.

Milton scraped the pine needles safely aside so that he could build a fire without setting fire to the woods. Milton searched the area for several stones large enough to ring the fire; it took a while, but at least the movement generated some warmth. The stones now in place, Milton gathered sticks for the fire. He cut a good supply of dried pine hearts so his fire would start easily and burn brightly.

At last ready to enjoy the fruits of his labor, he took from his backpack a small skillet and a piece of bacon for his supper. He could almost smell the bacon as he made ready to light the fire. He was filled with the sense of pride that only the truly independent can know. After all, what other 13-year-old could be so self-reliant?

He reached into his pocket for his box of waterproof matches and realized almost immediately that while the matches were waterproof, they weren't forget-proof. He searched everything in his possession and was unable to produce them. "Now what am I going to do?" he thought. Eventually, he decided to wrap himself in his quilt for the night and in the morning find someone with matches.

He had kept his composure, but still was unable to stop his teeth from chattering twenty-minutes later. He began to fear that he might freeze to death. He rose from his bed and walked quickly around the camp site, hoping the warmth would sustain him. But he could not ward off the cold. Finally, he was forced to consider the unthinkable: he would either have to go home or freeze to death. Only with the greatest reluctance did Milton gather his camping gear and begin the long, cold walk home.

On the way back, he was filled with embarrassment. He had made a defiant stand and had failed miserably. He wondered whether his family would laugh at his feeble efforts at manhood and independence. Would his grandfather make double-good on his promise to make his punishment more severe? Should he just apologize and get his punishment out of the way: even the warmth of the razor strap seemed somehow to outweigh the pain that it would inflict.

The way home was lit by a beautiful full moon, but a piercing cold wind blew from the north. Nearing his house, he was glad to see that the lights were on. For several moments, he stood outside the door, shivering in the cold, and wondering just what he would do and just how he would be received.

Then it occurred to him that he was in a position to help himself. What if he brought in the wood that he should have taken care of early that morning. From inside the house, there suddenly came the sound of wood being chopped and split.

So when Milton finally entered the house, his arms were full of wood for the cook stove. The rest of the family had just sat down to supper at the kitchen table. Finally, Milton mumbled apologetically, "I decided to cut the wood and bring it in." Without even looking up, his grandmother said, "Wash up; supper's ready." Grandpa just looked at Milton and said, talking to no one in particular, "It's kind of cold out there—regular hog-killing weather." Milton thought to himself, "Regular Milton-killing weather, too." The supper was delicious, but even more appreciated was the warmth from the old kitchen stove. But there was nothing to compare with the warmth he felt from again being in the midst of his caring family. No one said a word, then or later, about his immature behavior

Milton learned two important lessons on this day. The first, was never go camping without a pack of matches. But the most important thing he learned was what a wonderful grandfather he had—a grandfather who would deserve Milton's respect the rest of his life. Oh—and it was also the last time Milton ever ran away from home.

Chapter 10
The Paper Boy

Like most young men, Milton was always looking for ways to earn extra money. He mowed lawns, dug toilet pits, cut wood, trapped furs, and delivered papers. Each chore left him with special memories, but none more so than having his own paper route in Valdosta. When he first began the job, he didn't have a bicycle, so it goes without saying that he did a powerful lot of walking. Milton soon came to envy the other paper boys who delivered papers from their bikes. They were not only having fun riding their bikes, but they completed their routes far earlier than Milton could.

Though Milton very much wanted a bicycle, it simply was far beyond the financial means of his mother to provide. So he considered an option, and the name of that option "old Lightning," an old horse bought by Milton's grandfather at a livestock auction.

Grandpa Thompson was forever going to the sale barn to purchase mules, horses, or cattle for later resale, hoping to make a profit when the time was right. Lightning, a very old horse, was being fattened up by his grandfather so that he might look better and draw a few extra dollars at the sale in a few weeks. Lightning didn't even have a saddle, so Milton just rode him bareback on his paper route.

Apparently, Lightning was excited by his new work,

and that posed a problem for Milton. You see, Lightning was confined to the barn or pasture most of the time, so when he did get out, he very much wanted to run. But as an old horse unsure of his footing, he would sometimes stumble. Milton was afraid the horse might one day fall, but thought that he would be able to jump clear if Lightning's coordination failed him altogether.

One sunny afternoon around five o'clock, Milton and old Lightning started on their paper route. Lightning was feeling particularly frisky on this day. Milton was barely able to hold on before Lightning slowed, responding to Milton's voice and rein commands.

Milton rode up to the customer's porch and tossed a folded paper from the shoulder bag supplied to all paper boys. Soon, Milton began thinking that this was even better than having a bicycle: he didn't even have to peddle. But it didn't take long for him to change his mind, for it seemed all the dogs in Valdosta were chasing old Lightning. But the horse got in a few good kicks, and more than one dog was seen limping around the town for the next few days. In time, most wise Valdostan dogs gave up interest in old Lightning, and those few that persisted had to dodge one of the rocks Milton carried in his paper sack for just that reason. In a very short time, people came to welcome the sight of Milton and old Lightning. They no doubt reminded some of the older folks of their horse-riding days.

Better still, some of the young girls in Valdosta started talking with Milton as he made his rounds, petting the horse and exchanging conversation that Milton found most welcome. They began even to ask for horse rides. But Milton insisted that Lightning was strictly a "one-man" horse— wouldn't allow anyone else to ride him, especially girls. It was, of course, a white lie, but it worked.

For the most part, delivering papers with Lightning was a pleasure, and each day Milton found he was eagerly looking forward to his appointed rounds. But the excitement lasted only two weeks. For, on one cool, dark, rainy afternoon Milton and old Lightning left on their route, neither apparently in a very good mood. The cold rain probably caused Lightning to weigh the pros and cons of his new job, after all, there was something to be said for a warm stall and all the hay and oats one could eat.

At any rate, the constant rubbing of Milton's cold, wet bare-foot against the soft spot under Lightning's front legs began to irritate the horse. He would make a half-hearted attempt to unseat Milton, who somehow managed to hold on.

Horse and rider were understandably in a hurry to get out of the weather. Milton began taking short cuts across customers' lawns, with Lightning's six-inch hoof prints as evidence. Milton happened to be in the valley of Valdosta at the time, where it was the muddiest—and his customers, quite naturally, the angriest. So it was a choice of continuing to use old Lightning and losing customers or again walking his route. And while he was loyal to old Lightning, where money was concerned—well, loyalty would have to take a back seat.

Shortly thereafter, Milton's grandfather managed to sell old Lightning at an auction, though grandfather most likely presented him simply as "Lightning," rather than "old Lightning." Milton was truly sorry to see his friend go, but he knew his grandfather needed the money more than the horse.

Milton's paper boy days in Valdosta continued off and on for several years, keeping him busy and providing him with extra income. He looked forward to his route, where he would see his friends, get in an occasional fight, and even play a few games of baseball. Milton was far from an outstanding ballplayer, but he enjoyed the company of his friends, even if it did mean more than a few late deliveries.

One day while Milton was walking his route in lower Valdosta, he got into an argument with a boy called Red, who was about Milton's age. One thing led to another and Red took a swing at Milton and missed. Milton countered with a blow to Red's stomach, knocking the boy down. As Red got up, he grabbed a large rock and threw it at Milton. Fortunately for Milton, Red missed. Most unfortunately for Red, the rock did hit his father's cow, while his father was milking it. Cow, milk, stool, and father all flew in different directions when the rock hit. Red's father was soaked with milk and was seeing "red" in more ways than one.

He blamed Milton, and both father and son chased the paperboy from the area. Milton managed to escape, but his future deliveries to lower Valdosta were made from the far side of the road when passing Red's home.

One of Milton's most embarrassing moments as a newsboy came late one afternoon while delivering Mr. Carmichael's paper. Mr. Carmichael was a special customer to Milton because of Miss Carmichael, a girl Milton's age who Milton believed to be the prettiest girl ever born. She had long, golden hair and a beautiful face. And this was before Milton was old enough to include the female body into the equation. He was strictly a hair-and-face "man."

As much as Milton looked forward to the Carmichael delivery, it was his most difficult one. Each time the girl spoke to him, he became a tongue-tied stuttering and stammering fool. So he began to deliver the Carmichael's paper when the girl was not on the porch, even if it meant delivering it late. He would stretch out his conversation with another customer or, perhaps, stop at the store for an "extra-long" R.C. Cola until the girl would go inside her house.

One day Mr. Carmichael asked Milton to come around to the backyard, explaining that he had something he wanted Milton to see. Rounding the house, Milton stopped dead in his tracks. For there was his beloved, Jeraldine Carmichael, with, of all things, a pair of boxing gloves on her hands.

Apparently, the Joe Lewis craze (the Champ was from Alabama) had spread even to this girl, who belonged on a pedestal but surely not one with a ring around it. Milton had always thought that she knew how much he loved her and hoped she felt the same about him. But now Mr. Carmichael was asking Milton to slug it out at close quarters with the very girl that he worshipped from afar. It was hardly surprising that Milton didn't know what to do. He stammered some excuse so that he wouldn't have to hurt the one he loved. But Mr. Carmichael continued to goad Milton, calling him a sissy and making much noise about his being afraid to "spar" with Jeraldine. Milton had no idea what it meant to spar, but he soon found out.

Because there seemed no way out of it, the big bout between lover and beloved began. Milton intended to be a complete gentleman, directing only love taps in the direction of this soft, cuddly, and beautiful 12-year-old. To make a long story short, because Milton refused to mix it up with Jeraldine, she proceeded to beat him without mercy. Milton protected himself the best he could, covering up and shouting, "Stop it. Stop it." She was like a wildcat.

If she had failed to punch a single area of Milton's body, it wasn't for lack of effort. She even fouled him, and that did hurt.

Milton had been done in by the one he loved. But, then, when your opponent's father is the referee, what chance does one have? Anyway, Milton soon had second thoughts about the feminine charms of Jeraldine Carmichael. She certainly wasn't as nice as he had thought. And, perhaps, she was not so pretty after all. One thing Milton did know: the incident was easily the most embarrassing one in his young life—so embarrassing that he refused to tell his pals about it. Imagine. Getting beat up by a 12-year-old girl, or a girl of any age. For some things there are no excuses.

Chapter 11
School Days

Milton completed the Sixth Grade at Valdosta Grammar School and, at the age of 13, enrolled in Deshler High School in Tuscumbia. The transition was like hitting a brick wall. At Valdosta, he had been something of a teacher's pet. His favorite subject was recess, not surprising given his love for the outdoors. His favorite recess game was played near the school grounds, in a large ditch with high banks covered with kudzu vines. Milton and his playmates dug tunnels under the banks and would chase one another through the maze of vines and tunnels. They would return to class covered with dirt—but the teachers didn't seem to mind.

Deshler High School was a far more serious institution, where a student was actually expected to work hard and learn. Milton most enjoyed football, history, and library. He would check out several books from the library each week and would spend most of his time reading books of adventure, history, and exploration. But despite his enthusiasm, his grades were—well, terrible.

Two events that took place during physical education had a definite "impact" on Milton; both incidents involved football. During phys. ed., the teacher would split the class evenly into two teams and play football in the school yard. Milton, who could run very fast, broke free one day and the ball was thrown to him. All that remained was for him to run to the end of the field for a touchdown. Just before he reached the goal, he looked back to see how far behind he had left the pursuit. When he returned his head to the front, still running for all he was worth, he saw nothing but the trunk of a huge tree.

BUT HOW'S THE TREE?

Regaining consciousness in the principal's office, he remembered nothing after seeing the elm. Fortunately, he had suffered only bruises and minor facial cuts.

The second event occurred when, playing defensive back, he leaped for an interception, and the ball hit him square in the forehead. He immediately became dizzy and had difficulty seeing. He sat down on the bench and almost panicked when his vision began to turn gray. And then he lost his sight completely. He didn't tell anyone, because he couldn't believe it himself. But he had never been so afraid in his life. All types of thoughts raced through his throbbing head. Would he be selling pencils on street corners for the rest of his life, like that poor old blind man in Tuscumbia?

But his panic was premature; his vision began to clear

in about ten minutes, though to Milton it seemed like hours. For the next week, Milton stayed as far away from a football as he possibly could.

Back in Milton's days, lunch break was not nearly as structured as it now is. During the lunch hour, a student was free to spend it as he chose, as long as he returned for his next class. Milton often spent his lunch hour at the county courthouse, just a short distance from Deshler High. A statue dedicated to veterans of the Civil War stood at the front of the courthouse. Inside, Milton could watch a court in session or review the relics from the Civil War.

During one such trip to the courthouse, when he was downstairs in the bathroom, two men came in. They were members of a jury trying a man for moonshining: he had allegedly been caught in the act of making whiskey. Milton overheard one man say to the other that there was "no doubt" the accused was guilty. The other man, however, replied, "I know he is guilty, but he owes me over a hundred dollars for groceries charged at my store. If he goes to jail, I'll never collect that money."

The next day Milton read in the newspaper that the alleged moonshiner had been acquitted of the charge. He was only 13 at the time, but he was old enough to learn that there is more to law than what is written in the books.

During his year at Deshler High, Milton occasionally worked for a woman who owned and operated "Doc's Place," a small cafe. There he washed dishes and took orders from the rear section, where blacks were served. The blacks had to enter the cafe through a rear door and were seated at a rear counter hidden from view of those seated in the front. In return for washing the dishes, Milton received a free lunch. Usually, this consisted of a hamburger, a bowl of chili, and a glass of R.C. Cola. This worked well for Milton because a school lunch cost twenty cents.

One afternoon at Doc's, Milton took an order from a man, who ordered two hamburgers, a bowl of chili, and an R.C. Cola. His bill came to forty cents, which he paid with a five-dollar bill. Milton gave him his correct change, but the man demanded to speak to the manager. He told the manager that he had given Milton a twenty-dollar bill but had received change only for a five. Milton was both embarrassed and angry that someone would accuse him of stealing.

But Mrs. Jackson, the owner, immediately came to Milton's defense. She told the man that when change had to be made, it was Milton's responsibility to deliver the money to the person at the cash register, who then would make the correct change, and Mrs. Jackson was working the register that afternoon. She said the largest bill in the register was a ten. She accused the man of trying to steal by taking advantage of Milton's youth and threatened to call the police. The man did leave, muttering threats, and slamming the door behind him.

Milton missed very few days that school year, but, unfortunately, good attendance doesn't guarantee good grades. At the end of the year, Milton had failed Math and English; and barely passed History and Physical Education. Had he been given a grade for reading more books than any other student, he would have been given an A++. One of the teachers had taken an interest in him and told him that he was capable of doing much better if he would only apply himself. Milton knew very well that studying English and Math full-time would have taken time away from his independent reading, but, more importantly, from his hunting.

He had bought a single-shot .22 calibre rifle and spent

much of his study time hunting. As a result of pursuing his outside interests, Milton had failed the Seventh Grade and was forced to repeat it at Cherokee Vocational High School. He had heard that the classes were easier there. But it was just a rumor: he had to study harder.

Cherokee Vocational High School was seventeen miles from Milton's house. It was a country school—just an old, brick-wooden building constructed in a square. The outer section of the building, in which classes were held, had large windows; the interior section was used as an auditorium for assemblies.

When Milton first enrolled at Cherokee Vocational, he was given the option of entering Eighth Grade. But he refused the offer, telling the principal that he wanted to master Seventh Grade before moving on. Milton found that he enjoyed his new school and, soon, had read most of the "interesting" books in its library. But, again, he failed to "apply himself," and finished the year with a C average. But he had passed, and he was happy.

During the three years he attended Cherokee Vocational, Milton had several interesting experiences. In that time he made many close friends, whom he still remembers with great fondness after all of these years.

But Milton's years at Cherokee might have been better had it not been for the irritating habit—a habit that Grandpa Thompson had always been quick to point out—of always having the last word on everything. For example, one day the new principal came to Milton's English class to make an announcement. When the principal had finished and was leaving, Milton turned to a classmate and made a comment that was overheard by the principal.

The principal had just returned from the war. He had been in the Navy and had been severely wounded. As a result of his wounds, his hands trembled and his voice was shaky. He thought Milton was making fun of him, so he asked Milton to step outside into the hall with him. In the hall and out of view of the classroom, the principal grabbed Milton by his shirt and pushed him against the wall. "Kid," he said, "I've been through hell in the war, and I'm not going to take any sass from a smart-mouth kid. If I even see you looking at me wrong, I'm going to beat the hell out of you. Do you understand?"

Milton was speechless, but nodded his head to indicate that he did, indeed, understand. With that, the principal left Milton to do his own trembling. And the message took. For weeks after the incident, if Milton even saw the principal coming, he would distance himself as quickly as he could.

Not long after that incident, Milton found himself falling deeply in love. The girl was in most of his classes. As with most young teenage boys, Milton was reduced to a stammering simpleton in her presence. He once wrote her a note and gave it to another girl to be delivered. But the girl misunderstood; she thought the note, which Milton hadn't addressed, was for her. As a result, the would-be messenger thought that Milton had a crush on her. She began to follow him and was always extra-friendly. She was cute but not the object of Milton's affection. Because the two girls were such good friends, the situation became so hopelessly confused that Milton decided he would fall out of love.

While at Cherokee, Milton became involved in two fights. The first was started by a boy who sat behind him in English class and was always thumping him on the ear lobe. In addition to being painful, the thumping was distracting. And Milton certainly didn't need a distraction in English class! But the boy paid no heed to Milton's protests. Milton suffered the thumping for about a week. Then, one day he just turned in his chair and punched the boy as hard as he could, knocking both boy and desk to the floor. A furious fist-fight followed as Milton's classmates gathered to watch.

On this particular day, the class was being taught by a student-teacher. Shocked and young, she could only wring her hands and cry. Eventually, the fight was broken up by a few other boys. But Milton had taught his antagonist a lesson; he never bothered Milton again. And Milton felt good about having struck a good first blow; the fellow had it coming.

The second fight happened on the school bus that Milton rode 34 miles round-trip each day. To make the trip shorter, Milton would frequently read an exciting book. One day, on the way home from school, a boy began taunting Milton, calling him a book worm. Milton tried to ignore the boy, but his taunts continued. Finally, Milton closed his book and hit the boy in the stomach as hard as he could. The boy doubled over in pain, but recovered, and began fighting with Milton. Milton could see that, on the boy's right hand, he wore a large saddle ring. Milton did his best to duck the boy's punches and continued to pummel him in the stomach. But that ring struck Milton's head far more often than Milton would have liked.

Eventually, the bus driver stopped the bus and threw both boys off. Neither had any fight left in him; Milton had several large knots on his head, and his opponent had a very sore stomach. Together, they thumbed a ride home. That was the first and last fight between the two boys.

Though Milton didn't excel as a student, he still considered Cherokee Vocational a good school and wished he had applied himself better. He had participated in junior varsity football and track. He did well at both sports, but his first love was still as an outdoorsman.

And Milton had great respect for the teachers at Cherokee Vocational High School. Two he remembers with special fondness. Both were first-year teachers, and both were very pretty. Milton looked forward to running errands for these teachers. He would sometimes go into Cherokee for groceries, taking him away from school for an entire period.

Wood shop was one of Milton's favorite classes. Among his favorite projects were a magazine rack, several illegal fish traps, and a tool box. In the tool box, Milton constructed a secret compartment; it would be the perfect hiding place in the event he decided to steal something from the class. He filled the compartment with nails and kept them there for several days just to prove to himself that they would be undetected. However, when he took the box home, it no longer had the nails.

Milton's shop teacher (who was bald and, therefore, considered "ancient" by Milton), decided to sell candy and Cokes to his students to raise money for supplies. Predictably, the stealing of candy and Cokes became something of a game for the boys. The easiest way, they found, was for a few boys to divert the teacher's attention while others stole the goodies from the refreshment counter.

However, Milton, never participated in any of these "games." He had been raised by his mother and grandfather to respect the property of others. Incidentally, the shop teacher Milton thought was "ancient" still looked the same twenty years later.

Chapter 12
The BB Gun Battle

On Christmas day of 1942, about one-half of the boys in Valdosta received Red Ryder BB guns. Everywhere the boys went, the BB guns went with them—everywhere, that is, except to school or church. Imagine the reaction today if 10 to 15 boys were seen walking around with BB guns. Most likely, the police would be called. But, in those days, a boy and his BB gun was an accepted fact of life. It was considered training for the .22 calibre rifle that would come later.

After the Christmas of 1942, birds were developing nervous disorders from the onslaught of BBs from every direction. Cats and chickens were also suffering from heightened awareness. Overall, the boys were responsible with their weapons, but fathers sometimes found in necessary to take the guns from sons who showed no respect for safety. Over the months, Milton and friends became such good shots that they could light a kitchen match from ten feet.

Now it happened that each Saturday afternoon, the boys from Valdosta would gather in the meadow below Sugar Hill, shoot their BB guns, and play ball. Back in those days, that ordinary meadow seemed endless. One Saturday afternoon, a boy from Sugar Hill showed up and started an argument with a Valdosta boy. The argument soon became a wrestling match and a few blows were exchanged. The lad from Sugar Hill left, but returned about a half-hour later with a few of his friends, all armed with BB guns. They opened fire on the Valdosta "gang," hitting several of them. Being hit by a BB is like being stung by a wasp. Milton was struck at least four times before he was able to get to his rifle and begin firing back. Soon, BBs were whizzing in both directions, and boys cried out as they were hit. The boys were abandoning one cover for another to escape the barrage.

One of the boys from Sugar Hill had an unfair advantage. He had a Daisy BB gun, a pump-type that could be primed, giving the BBs from his rifle more power than those fired from the Red Ryders. Being hit by a BB from the Daisy "pump" was a nasty experience, as Sid, one of the Valdosta boys, found out. The BB struck him in the corner of the eye. When the Valdosta boys noticed how badly Sid had been hurt, they all directed their fire toward the kid with the Daisy rifle.

Sometime later, the boy with the powerful BB gun would relate that he had been struck more than thirty times with BBs from the Valdosta group. Meanwhile, the battle raged for almost an hour with neither side willing to concede defeat.

The battle finally ended when David, one of the older Valdosta boys, happened to pass by. He borrowed Milton's BB gun and charged the Sugar Hill group. He disarmed some of them and caused the rest to flee. David's brave charge really impressed Milton. Sid was the only real casualty, but the BB had lodged in the corner of his eye near his nose, causing pain but no visual damage.

The "Battle of Sugar Hill" was won by Valdosta and, for several years, there was animosity between the two rival groups. After a time, however, as the boys grew older, friendships evolved. This happened because time is a great healer, but also because some of those Sugar Hill boys had pretty sisters, making it easier to let bygones be bygones.

That Sugar Hill battle is, of course, nowhere recorded, but to those young boys involved in it, it was never forgotten. The confrontation helped develop character and was a test of bravery. But, to the participants, perhaps the greatest lesson was that a good ball game is more enjoyable—and infinitely less painful.

Chapter 13
Boy Scouts

When Milton was 12, he joined the newly organized Boy Scout Troop in Valdosta. He was thrilled; being a member of the scouts would mean a lot of outdoor adventures with his friends. He had heard that scouting was a fine experience; it taught sportsmanship and even handy things to know, like how to tie different kinds of knots. The scouts met once a week, but it was not all business. The boys found time to play games of chase and "seize the bacon." The meetings were held at the Valdosta Grammar School, located near Highway 72, the main route between Cherokee and Tuscumbia.

For Milton, scouting proved to be exciting for two reasons: first, the fun of the games and the crafts; second, the greater excitement of the activities after the scout master had departed. It seemed that after every scout meeting, there would be a fight between boys from Valdosta and Sugar Hill. There had been "bad blood" between them ever since the infamous BB gun "Battle of Sugar Hill." Not that the guys from Sugar Hill were all bad. It's just that boys will be boys and rivals will be rivals.

Of all the animosity, none was greater than that between the Hamm boy from Sugar Hill and the Doby boy from Valdosta. Milton liked both boys and tried hard to keep from taking sides. Neither Doby, the younger of the two rivals, nor Hamm was about to turn his back on a good fight. Doby had brothers, but they had always remained out of the dispute, until one day the Hamm boy slandered the entire Doby family. After that, the fights became something more than child's play and led to the disbanding of the scout troop six months after it was formed. Milton had passed his second-class scout test and was disappointed that he wouldn't be able to continue.

Before the brawl that led to the disbanding of the troop, the boys were having fun in another way after the meetings. It was still war-time—1944-1945, and times were hard. Everything was rationed, and nothing more so than automobile tires.

Milton and several friends (no doubt influenced by the older boys) decided to "help" travelers along Highway 72 overcome the tire shortage. The boys found old tires that appeared sound, at least on one side. Next, a visit was made to the nearest outhouse, where a "collection" was taken and smeared on the tires with a brush. The tires were then placed on Highway 72 as "bait."

The spot chosen for this dirty trick was a section of the highway with a 12-foot-high bank, obviously affording the pranksters some protection from the irate motorists who were sure to follow. The boys would then place the "treated" tire on the highway and await their first victim. Because tires were so scarce, almost everyone fell for the trick. And because they were up to their mischief after scouting—between 9 and 10 PM—there were fewer travelers, operating on the theory that the fewer enemies one makes the better.

The typical motorist would pass the tire, slam on his brakes, and back up to it. They would quickly get out of their cars and grab the tire, hoping to toss it in their trunk before another traveler came by. But the motorists did not keep the tire in their hands for long. The "scouts" hiding up the bank were treated to a different tirade of obscenities each week. And talk about audacity—many times the boys would yell, "Mister, please put the tire back on the road." And believe it or not, most of the motorists would do just that. Motorists would then drive about a mile to the nearest service station to wash their hands and let the service-station manager know what they thought of the boys of Valdosta. But the tire-smearing stopped when scouting was disbanded.

Milton often wondered whether the scout master knew anything of what happened after he left each week. But Milton honestly appreciated the efforts of the scout master to bring the merits of scouting to his area. In the brief time that he was a scout, Milton learned much that would serve him well in later life.

Chapter 14
Making Sorghum Molasses

When Milton was ten, he was asked by his grandfather to help in the care of the sorghum-cane crop, which is used to make molasses, widely used by farm families as a sweetener. Milton watched with great interest as his grandfather planted two acres of seed that came in as cane. The cane that grew along the stream banks could also be used as fishing poles, and Milton was looking forward to two acres of fishing poles. He was disappointed when his grandfather explained that sorghum cane is a source of molasses, and makes for a poor fishing rod.

When the cane had grown to about six feet, Milton could cut down a shoot and divide it into sections that he jammed into the pockets of his overalls. This way, he could enjoy a sweet snack anytime he wanted. All he had to do was chew on the cane, and a tasty juice would flow. Anyone who wanted to find Milton could have done so simply by following the pieces of chewed cane. Even his dog, Jigs, enjoyed chewing on the cane.   One of the games that Milton most enjoyed was sword-fighting. He and his friends would make wooden swords and play pirate, just like the movie actors. Often, they would spend an entire afternoon sword-fighting.

One day in August, Milton noticed his grandfather cutting and whittling several two-foot wooden swords. At first, Milton wondered whether his grandfather was intending to join the boys in their pirate games. But the swords that he was whittling seemed to Milton so sharp that they could easily cut someone.

It didn't take Milton long to discover why his grandfather had whittled the swords. One day he called Milton and two of his playmates and asked them if they would like to "attack enemy soldiers" that were out in the field. He took the boys to the cane field and told them they could cut the leaves from the sorghum cane. He explained that before making sorghum molasses, the leaves had to removed to allow the juice to flow from the cane.

Well, the "attack" on the cane field was fun, for the first hour. But the remaining three hours were pure misery, and by the time the last sorghum leave had been severed, the boys were barely able to lift their arms. The only reason they persisted was because Milton's grandfather had promised the boys a cold watermelon when the job was finished. And, oh, how they enjoyed their reward!

The following day, Milton and his grandfather used long, machete-type knives to cut the cane, then loaded it onto a wagon, a job that took most of the day. They chained the cane in place for the trip to the molasses-making equipment at the bank of Smith Creek at Underwood Mountain.

Milton's Uncle Addison had grown up at Smith Creek, and Milton had spent many hours there hunting and fishing with his uncle. So he was really looking forward to the following day when he would accompany his grandfather on the wagon to Smith Creek.

Smith Creek was especially interesting because Indians had lived in that area, and many Indian artifacts could be found in the meadow adjacent to the creek. Uncle Addison could remember, as a young man, plowing up human bones and arrow heads as he helped his father farm the field. Sometimes, Milton, too, wished that he lived back in the days when Smith Creek was Indian territory.

That night, Milton was barely able to sleep. His grandfather woke him at dawn, and they sat down to a breakfast of homemade sausage, hot biscuits, and eggs. The day was already hot and muggy as Milton helped his grandpa harness the team of mules. The wagon was packed so high with cane that it was difficult for the two to climb atop the load. The trip was about six miles and would take more than two and a half hours.

About at the half-way point, they stopped at a spring frequently used by travelers as a place to get a cold drink and to water the team. Someone had left an old dipper at the spring that was used by everyone to drink from. While the mules were drinking, Milton climbed down from the cane to get a drink, then passed the dipper up to his grandfather. Milton never found anything as refreshing as cold spring water.

When they arrived at Smith Creek, they drove the team to an area where three large metal pans were mounted on a rock frame, with space under the frames for building a fire to heat the pans, thus cooking the cane juice. Each pan was about three-feet wide, six-feet long and six-inches deep. A grinder, which extracted the juice from the cane, was located about thirty feet from the pans. The cane was then stacked next to the grinder, and it was Milton's job to feed the cane to the grinder, which was turned by a mule harnessed to a long pole. The mule could be urged on by a swat from a tree limb. As the cane was pushed into the turning grinder, the juice would pour from a spout into a bucket. When enough juice had been collected and poured into the pans, the juice was boiled into a thick syrup.

An old gentleman, who owned the processing equipment, was on hand to assist with cooking the molasses. For the use of his equipment, he received a small share of the output. The old man was considered by everyone to be an expert molasses-maker, and he knew just how long to cook the juices. Milton learned that molasses are rated by color. If the juice is allowed to cook too long, it becomes too dark and stronger than normal. This product is known as blackstrap molasses. Molasses cooked to a color resembling that of tea, Milton learned, is considered the best and is most in demand.

The hot August day passed slowly. When Milton had finished feeding the grinder, he was allowed to walk around, exploring the stream bank. The water was very shallow, flowing clean and clear over a thick bed of gravel. Milton cooled off in one of the deepest areas of the stream.

Milton's grandfather had brought along several

sausage biscuits for lunch. They were so hungry that not a crumb remained, washing down their food with a cool drink from Smith Creek. When his grandfather went back to work, Milton made a small bow from a cedar limb and several arrows from weeds. He usually carried shoe laces in his pocket if he ever had need to tie something, and one of these laces he used as a bow string. He then spent the rest of the afternoon shooting at snakes, lizards, and birds. He did kill a few lizards, but missed the snakes and birds.

Just before the sun set, Milton's grandfather said that the time had come to go, and he got no argument from Milton, who was very tired and more than ready to go. His grandfather said they had processed 12 gallons of molasses. Milton slept for most of the ride home, lying on some old burlap bags that were in the wagon bed.

All that winter Milton enjoyed eating the molasses, and he took pride in his role in preparing it. And he was especially glad that his grandfather had trusted him to be part of the molasses-processing crew. It was an experience that he would always cherish.

Chapter 15
Thanksgiving Gathering

Of all the things that Milton enjoyed about Thanksgiving, he most enjoyed having his cousins, aunts, and uncles together at grandpa's house. Thanksgiving dinner would be served around one o'clock, but he would have several hours to enjoy the company of his cousins. They would play ball, or games of chase, and, in general, just horse around. As they grew older, they would go squirrel or rabbit hunting.

For dinner, the kitchen would be crowded, but no one seemed to mind. Milton's youngest cousins would be seated at side tables, and his little sister, Frieda, would sit next to him on a two-gallon lard can, which positioned her perfectly at the table and made her feel more "grown up." She was always dressed in a cute little starched cotton dress. She would sit quietly, but expectantly, waiting for "Papa Thompson" to give the blessing so that dinner could begin.

After the blessing, the Thompson kin got down to the serious business of eating and conversation. Though times were hard, there was never a lack of food. A typical Thanksgiving dinner would include roast pork shoulder, roast chicken with cornbread stuffing, sweet potatoes, green beans, cornbread, and cranberry sauce. To drink, there was milk, iced tea, lemonade, and coffee. Though the roast pork was always a hit, the roasted chicken was not one of Milton's favorites. And for good reason. For it was Milton's pre-Thanksgiving responsibility to choose the rooster that would be the "main course" and to be its executioner.

In selecting the "main course," Milton's main consideration was based on the rooster's previous behavior. Some of the roosters had long, sharp spurs growing from the backs of their feet, and some of these often amused themselves by chasing Milton and his sister and spurring them. For this very good reason, Milton's sister was reluctant to play in the yard where the roosters were.

When he could put it off no longer, Milton would scatter corn and summon the chickens. There, he would hold court and decide which of the roosters had been the year's worst offender. It seemed to Milton that each of the roosters approached the corn with something of a guilty conscience and with some knowledge that this day was somehow a special day. Each rooster presented himself as best he could and, thereafter, did its best to avoid capture. But usually it was a Rhode Island Red that had been the worst offender and would be chosen to make the supreme sacrifice.

With the condemned rooster finally captured, Milton next had to decide how best to execute it. He could either wring its neck or sever it with an ax. If the rooster had been guilty of only minor misdemeanors during the year, Milton would make the execution quick and painless at the chopping block. But if the rooster had been a year-long "felon," it would have its neck twisted, with Milton deriving some satisfaction remembering the pain of the spurrings. But, with either method, Milton had little appetite for chicken on Thanksgiving Day.

After dessert—usually sweet-potato or apple pie—the men and women went their different directions: the women to clean up and wash dishes, then to talk about whatever it is that women talk about; the men to gather on the porch for a smoke and manly conversation. This conversation, more often than not, took the direction of how the younger generation was "going to the dogs," meaning far more lazy and sassy that they had been.

But all Milton knew was that, after Thanksgiving dinner, his "generation" didn't go to the dogs, but to the Government Reservation, where they played Cowboys and Indians. Those were good times, Milton now often remembers. There was no television and the radio was turned on only for special programs. The boys used to listen to Gene Autry, "The Green Hornet," and "The Shadow." Milton's grandma would listen to "Young Widow Brown," "When a Girl Marries," and a few other programs as she ironed and did other household chores.

Each evening, Milton's grandfather listened to the news. He insisted on quiet so that he might hear Gabriel

Heater's news of the day. The only time Milton heard his grandfather swear was when President Roosevelt would deliver his "Fireside Chats." Grandpa would yell, "Turn that _____ off!"

Life was so simple back then. Drinking, swearing, and indecent behavior weren't considered acceptable behavior. Decent people were looked up to; indecent people looked down on. And the state of one's character was well known and closely monitored for change in a small town like Valdosta. Back then, what people thought of you mattered. Milton often marvels at how drastically things have changed, and is glad that he lived in the times of decency—the times that were never to be repeated.

Chapter 16
Halloween

Of all the holidays and special days on the calendar, Milton and his friends enjoyed Halloween the most—at least until Christmas. Not that they would do harmful things, but it was a time to prowl, a time for "boys to be boys" and get away with it. The nights were crispy cool, and Milton and his pals felt like doing something different. Halloween, after all, does come only once a year, they reasoned. At first, it was fun going trick-or-treating, but as they grew older (some boys were already taller than their fathers) it became embarrassing to tower over someone and say, "trick or treat."

There were other, "more mature," things that might be done on Halloween night. There were always a few special folks that deserved special treatment. Again, nothing harmful, but just enough to make those people aware that "they had been noticed."

Mr. Hamby always seemed to be a favorite target. Not that any of the boys had a particular dislike for him, but because he had a set of lawn furniture hewn from trunks of old chestnut trees: a table and three chairs. It was the furniture that was the special target. The table and chairs were very heavy and painted white. Every Halloween, Mr. Hamby's furniture would disappear and later be found somewhere in Valdosta where one might least expect to find it. One year, the boys carried it to the roof of someone's house; another year, it had been hidden in a pig pen or hen house. But always it would take Mr. Hamby days to locate the missing pieces. Mr. Hamby's disappearing furniture became an annual event in Valdosta, and Mr. Hamby was always a good sport about it.

There was another man in Valdosta who was not at all liked by Milton and his friends, and each Halloween they would always find a novel way of getting back at him. One of the tricks they pulled on this man was to take a large paper bag and fill it about one-quarter full of manure—fresh, soft, smelly manure. A volunteer from among the boys would quietly place the bag near the man's front door as the other boys watched from a roadside ditch. The volunteer then lit the bag, waited till it was fully afire, and rang the doorbell just before making a mad dash to the ditch to watch with his companions.

The man opened the door, immediately saw the burning bag, and began tramping on it to put the fire out. He was wearing a pair of loose house slippers. One of the slippers came off in his wild stomping, and his bare foot was smeared with manure. If his language was a fair indication, the man was enraged, so Milton and the boys decided it was time to put some real distance between themselves and their target.

In the days that followed, the man tried very hard to learn the identities of the culprits. While no one volunteered any information, Milton still felt strongly that the man had a pretty good idea which Valdosta youths had "gone to the dogs" that night.

Milton had always disliked drive-by trick-or-treaters who would toss eggs—or worse—at houses. This was a common prank each year. To the best of Milton's knowledge, this cowardly trick was the work of outsiders; he believed that the boys of Valdosta were above such destructive pranks. Rotten eggs were difficult to clean from wood siding and would always leave a stain—to say nothing of the odor.

One Halloween, the older boys of the neighborhood "borrowed" a farmer's wagon and reassembled it atop the flat roof of the two-story Lily Pond General Store, operated by Uncle Ned Hovatar. On the morning after Halloween, folks driving down Highway 72 were treated to the sight of a completely assembled farm wagon on top of the roof. Everyone seemed to find it amusing—everyone, that is, except the owner of the wagon. None of the boys had a grudge against that farmer; he was a victim for no other reason than that he happened to own a wagon that was convenient to "borrow."

The farmer had to disassemble his wagon and remove it one piece at a time. Several people volunteered to help him, including some of the boys who were responsible for the wagon being on the roof in the first place. The farmer never knew for certain just who was involved in the prank, but Milton thought he had a pretty good idea. However, once the wagon was reassembled and back on the farm, the farmer probably thought it was pretty funny himself. Milton made a bet with several of his friends that no one would ever again be able to take the farmer's wagon. And he was right.

That same Halloween, a group of boys somehow managed to get a cow onto the second floor of the Tuscumbia Grammar School. Cows do not like walking down stairs, and the principal of the school had a very difficult time forcing the creature from the building. But the school's janitor had a more difficult time cleaning up the mess left by the cow, who, it would seem, had reason to be distressed.

Then there was the Halloween that Milton sneaked up to a front porch to "borrow" a piece of heavy porch furniture that he planned to hide. It was close to nine at night, and as he cautiously approached the darkened house, he was surprised that the owner had retired so early, making his job that much easier. He would simply snatch the chair and take it up the road to another house and hide it in a hen house.

But just as Milton reached for the chair, he was startled by a noise at the side of the house—sort of a metallic click. Before he could move, the owner of the house, who happened to be home after all, fired six shots into the air from his revolver. Milton had no trouble seeing each of the six shots flare against the night sky. Nor did he have any trouble getting his skinny legs to carry him as far from that house as they possibly could. The sudden shock understandably diluted Milton's Halloween spirit, and he decided to go home early—actually, quite early, because he ran the whole way, checking over his shoulder every few yards.

Halloween night of 1945 was, as far as Milton was concerned, a classic. He met his pals in the valley to determine what memorable act of mischief—other than taking Mr. Hamby's furniture—they might commit. He arrived to find that plans had already been made.

Milton was told that the plot for the night was to roll an old car, side over side, down the hill and to position it under the overhang of the store, upside down. They would have to move the old car more than a quarter of a mile, but they did so, taking their time and being careful not to attract attention—not so easily done on Halloween night.

Fortunately, there were only a few cars on the road late in the evening, and they had the car in position in about an hour. While they were moving the car, they gathered up old tires, scrap—anything they could find to completely fill the space under the overhang.

Early the next morning, most of the teen population of Valdosta had gathered at the store; they wouldn't have missed the reaction of the owner for the world. He drove up, parked his car, then sat there for quite sometime. He got out of his car and entered the store through the back door, never saying a word. A short time later, he returned to his car and turned on the radio. He sat listening, looking for all the world like a man without a care in the world. Milton and the rest of the pranksters were puzzled beyond words.

Twenty minutes later, two men arrived in a large truck and hoisted the car out from under the store front. Next, they loaded it onto the truck along with the rest of the scrap the boys had collected. The driver of the trunk went up to the store owner, handed him some money, and thanked him for the scrap. After the truck drove away, the owner of the store turned to the boys and thanked them for giving him "all that scrap" to sell: it had brought twenty-three dollars and sixty cents.

In their obsession with trickery, Milton and his friends had forgotten that a nation at war desperately needs scrap metal and old tires. They themselves had earned money selling the very items that they had used in their prank. The joke, it seemed, was on them. Twenty-three dollars and sixty cents was a lot of money in 1945. Farm laborers were only earning one-to-four dollars a day.

The owner of the store, either because he was a good person or, perhaps, to "rub it in," treated the boys to free R.C. Colas and moon pies. The boys ate but did not really enjoy the treat, knowing now that they had been out-smarted.

But the story doesn't really end there. For the man had been preparing to dig footings for an addition to the store. Milton and his friends had carelessly removed the markers that had been carefully placed for the new structure. But the money that the man had made on the scrap more than made up for the damage they had caused by pulling up the survey stakes.

Halloween tricks back then weren't limited to planned antics. When cherry bombs became widely available, Milton and his "co-conspirators" pooled their money together and bought several, along with some large fire crackers. Oh, how they enjoyed sneaking up to a porch and throwing a cherry bomb. Other favorite tricks were soaping windows and exploding fire crackers in mail boxes. These they called their "hit-and-run" tactics.

During the forties, there were many teenagers of about the same age living in Valdosta. The ol' valley must have seemed quite dull when most of those boys left for the service or, simply, to seek their fortunes elsewhere. It was a time never to be forgotten by those who lived through the era.

Chapter 17
Squirrel Hunting

To people living in the cities, or in the suburbs, squirrels seem more like pets than creatures of the wild. But the squirrels in the country are far from tame. In the country, squirrels fear humans and are difficult to locate. That is why squirrel hunting (particularly the grey and fox squirrels) is such a favorite pastime of rural dwellers. Squirrel has been an important part of country cooking for generations. It is most often served fried or stewed, but squirrel cooked just about any way is acceptable. It is not hard to understand, then, given the excitement of the hunt and the delicacy of the meal, why squirrel-hunting season was so popular in the country.

Milton was obsessed with squirrel hunting. During season (and, admittedly, out of it), he chased the elusive squirrel. Sometimes he would come home empty-handed, having been out-witted by the elusive creatures —but not always.

One cold November day, Milton went squirrel hunting with his .22 calibre Stevens rifle on the Government Reservation near Spring Creek, about a mile from his home. Arriving at the bank of Spring Creek, where several large oak trees grew, he met two older hunters from the town of Tuscumbia. Milton knew both men and asked if he could hunt with them, but they decided they didn't want a 13-year-old tagging along.

One of the men told Milton they had just spotted a large

squirrel in the tree they were standing under, and suggested that Milton might want to linger awhile to see if he could shoot it. The man said it was one of the biggest squirrels he had ever seen.

The gullible Milton believed the tale and was only too happy to take up a position beneath the tree and wait for the squirrel to resume his acorn hunt. Milton waited for twenty minutes and still no squirrel. He was just about ready to abandon his watch when he sighted, not one, but two grey squirrels feeding in the top of the tree. He shot them both and was preparing to take them home to be cleaned and for his grandmother to cook. They would be tastier than fried chicken.

Just as Milton was ready to leave, the men returned and saw Milton holding the two dead squirrels. They asked where he had found them, and Milton said, "Why, right where you said. In this tree." And he thanked them for the tip. The men just looked at each other and laughed. They walked off shaking their heads and still laughing. And Milton noticed that neither had killed a squirrel. Only then did it occur to Milton that the men had been putting him on. And, at the same time, it dawned on him that the joke had been on them.

Though squirrel hunting was serious business in the country, it was not without its humorous moments. Because there were so many hunters in the woods during squirrel season, Milton and a friend decided to have some fun. They took the tail from a very large—and long dead—fox squirrel and climbed, at great risk, a tall oak, nailing the tail to the top of a large limb with most of the tail showing. From the ground it would appear that a large squirrel was on top of the limb in a hole with its tail hanging over the edge.

After several weeks, the limb had nearly been shot off by hunters who had sworn they were shooting at the biggest fox squirrel in the area. Finally, both the limb and the tail had been blasted to shreds.

Milton got more than he bargained for on one of his squirrel hunts. Not far from his home, there was a hill with many large acorn trees and a substantial squirrel population. One day, he spotted a large fox squirrel feeding at the top of a tree. Milton slipped as close to the tree as he could without alerting the squirrel, and shot and wounded it. It is an unwritten rule of the woods never to leave wounded game to suffer.

Unable to see the squirrel, Milton did see fur sticking out from a limb and shot his .22 rifle at the limb where the wounded squirrel had taken refuge. Without realizing it, the angle of his rifle caused the shots to pass over a home at the edge of the woods belonging to an old black women. Even at a distance, Milton could hear her yelling at him. But Milton continued firing each time he saw the fur move; and the woman continued yelling.

He must have fired ten rounds over the house: each time he fired, he could hear the "zing" of the bullets flying through the air. Soon, he heard the woman yell, "White folks, I done told you to stop shooting over my house, and you won't listen." Then, to Milton's surprise and considerable fright, the lady fired two shotgun blasts over his head. He heard the pellets shredding the leaves; twigs and leaves were falling at his feet.

This was enough to cause Milton to abandon the hunt, unwritten law or no unwritten law. He took off for home as fast as a 13-year-old boy under attack might be expected to. It was some time before Milton dared hunt in that area again. In was an important lesson, but one necessary for him to learn.

Chapter 18
The BeeTree

Milton had been reading a book about how Indians lived before the white man came to the New World. He was impressed by how the native Americans used maple sugar and honey as sweeteners. Milton didn't know anything about maple sugar, but he did know that bees were everywhere present. And had removed enough stingers from his body to know this. From the book, Milton learned the Indians would find a place where bees watered, and then follow the bees back to their hive. Milton decided to try this; he might just hit the mother lode of honey. Milton had tasted honey before from friends of his family who kept bees. Honeycomb was delightful to chew. It was sweet and lasted longer than chewing gum. Honeycomb was also called bees' wax, and was used for many things.

Wild bees built their hives in hollow trees, cliff sides, holes in rocks, and in abandoned farms and houses. Milton decided to walk back to the mountains, locate a spring, and attempt to follow the bees to their hive. If the method was good enough for the Indians and the early pioneers, it would be good enough for Milton.

Milton walked about two miles back into a ridge behind the farm to a spring that flowed from the base of a cliff. He sat for several minutes but didn't have long to wait:

bees were, indeed, flying to and from the spring. But he soon realized it was all but impossible to follow a single bee any great distance. After several hours of watching and pondering, a system occurred to him that might allow him to trace the bees back to their hive. He watched the flight of a bee until he could no longer see it; he lost sight of it near a tree. He then walked to that tree and waited for another bee to pass. It worked. Each bee was leading him closer and closer to the hive.

Milton had to be careful because the ground was uneven, and there was the constant danger of stepping on a rattlesnake. He had the feeling he was keeping one eye on the bee and the other on the ground, but he was making progress. His worst fear almost came true when he stepped on a large black racer—not a rattlesnake but a sudden jolt to his nervous system nonetheless. But the racer was as frightened of Milton as Milton was of it, and the two quickly parted company.

He lost sight of the bee he'd been following, but sat and waited for another to come along. As he waited, Milton just happened to notice a large white oak tree with a hole in the trunk about ten feet above the ground. To state the matter simply, the hole was abuzz with bees. Again Milton sat to consider the best way to get the honey that must surely be in the hollow of the tree. He remembered reading that the Indians would build a fire to smoke the bees from their hive. But, because the hole seemed too far above the ground to reach, he could see no way that he might smoke them out.

But he had come this far, and thought too much of his outdoor skills to be out-witted by bees. So he began piling flat rocks at the base of the oak. When the pile reached a height of six feet, Milton began his climb; but the closer to the hole he got, the angrier the bees got. He was strung several times before he decided that it might be wise to let both bees and pursuer take a rest. And the bee stings had weakened his resolve somewhat.

The tree, about four-feet in diameter, was quite large in comparison with other trees in the immediate area. Growing impatient, Milton decided to risk a quick glance to see if the hole contained any honey, and was immediately stung on his forehead for his foolish impatience. His face would eventually swell into a grotesque mask. Admitting defeat, at least for this day, Milton decided to return home and have his grandmother treat his many stings with, of all things, snuff spit, which was the best home-remedy yet developed.

The honey in that old oak became something of an obsession with Milton, and he made one more trip in an attempt to smoke the bees out. This, too, failed, and he decided he was going to need help. He talked with one of his buddies, Elroy Cabaniss, who would always spend time with Milton when his farm chores permitted. Elroy, too, was enthusiastic about the idea because he loved honeycomb, but he wasn't so sure he wanted to cut down a large oak just to get at the honey. But Milton worked hard to change his mind by telling him just how easy it would be to relieve the bees of their honey once the tree was on the ground.

In talking about the matter, they soon realized that far more planning would have to go into their effort before they would be successful: equipment such as onion sacks to be placed over their straw hats to protect their heads; long-sleeved shirts, strings to tie their trouser legs shut; and cotton gloves to protect their hands. Should they find the honey, they would need a washtub and two two-gallon buckets. Also, they included in the plans an axe and a saw for cutting the tree down.

They boys finally arrived at the tree one hot Saturday afternoon. They were already tired from the walk in the heat. They sat a good thirty feet from the tree for an early lunch of sardines and crackers. Both were thinking that the honey from the tree would make a perfect dessert. So close but, yet, so far.

It was now time for action; the tree would have to be felled. It appeared to be hollow, and they hoped to make quick work of it. Four-hours later, they were still cutting away at what proved to be one solid oak tree. The axe and saw were both dull, which didn't make their work any easier. They were getting blisters and their tempers were running short, but they persisted. Their heavy clothing had become both a boon and a bane: they were protected from the dive-bombing bees but they were so hot inside the clothes that their energy was quickly being sapped. When it seemed they could go on no longer, they heard the tree crack and watched as it toppled to the ground.

Both boys and bees were wildly excited, but for totally different reasons. The bees had surrounded the boys in a huge swarm, but so far their protection was holding. Now the question was how to remove the honey. If they thought they had worked hard cutting the tree down, they now discovered that their work had just begun. For the only way to get at the honey was to split the fallen tree, which would be harder than felling and it was.

To keep the bees at a distance, Milton and Elroy built a fire and covered it with damp grass; the smoke would keep the bees away. But the smoke was a hazard to the boys as well as the bees. When they had finally finished splitting the tree, they could not believe how much honey and honeycomb the hollow of the tree contained. The hollow was the size of a barrel. They could also see that if they had sawed four inches higher on the tree, their work would have been much easier; there was only some six inches of wood surrounding the honey.

The boys couldn't have been any happier how handsomely their efforts had repaid them. Before leaving the tree—their washtub and two two-gallon buckets filled with honey—they reclosed that part of the tree, hoping to induce the bees to make more honey. But bees are smarter than boys give them credit for. When Milton and Elroy returned to the tree the next summer, the bees had abandoned the fallen tree.

If they thought they had worked hard getting the honey, carrying the honey back home was the real chore. At least they could remove the oppressive protective clothing they had worn. While a stray bee would, on occasion, fly up from the honey and sting one of the unwary boys, they would still be glad to be rid of the furnace that the clothes had become. And Milton and Elroy probably would have felt sorry for stealing the bees' honey had it not been for those occasional stings. They compensated for the pain with a bite from the delicious honeycomb. When they finally arrived home, they felt like returning Civil War heroes.

No one could remember seeing such a vast amount of honey from a single bee hive. Milton and Elroy shared the glory of the honey and the glory of the praise from their families and friends. The honeycomb lasted several weeks. As for the next assault on a honey tree—well, that's another story for another time.

Chapter 19
Blackberries and Snakes

Like most southern boys, Milton had a healthy respect for snakes. Not that they were anything special—he was, after all -a country boy—but it was always wise to avoid stepping on them if one wanted to keep his heart pounding in regular rhythm.

Milton had his share of snake encounters in his young life, and he learned early that an angry snake hisses. A few even beat the ground with their tails when angry. When you spent as much time in the woods and around the water as Milton had, you tend to know snakes. Consequently, Milton would frequently caution his friends to be careful when they were out with him.

Milton was always looking for ways to earn money. A Mr. White, who lived in an apartment attached to the general store at Lily Pond, asked Milton one day to pick ten gallons of blackberries that he was going to use to brew blackberry wine. He offered Milton one dollar for each gallon of berries, clearly an offer too good to pass up. Milton had often worked all day chopping or picking cotton and seldom earned over three or four dollars.

During blackberry season, the best and largest berries were found in river and creek bottoms. Milton knew of a place on the Tennessee River where the berries grew very large. The only problem was that the area along the river was thick with brush and snake-infested. And those snakes grew large in the bottom lands where there was plenty of cover and plenty of food.

Because of the threat posed by the snakes, Milton asked his friend Harold to help him, agreeing to split the money with him. Milton was looking for safety—and, perhaps, a bit of courage—in numbers as they penetrated the thick brush along the river bottom. The boys armed themselves with long sticks that they would use for making "good snakes" (as in, the only good snake is a dead snake) of any that happened to get underfoot. As the blackberry picking progressed, several snakes were shown the way to "good-snake heaven." Picking berries under such conditions is certainly no, er, picnic, but the boys pushed on.

The buckets were almost full when Milton reached for a row of especially large berries. As he reached, he heard a hissing noise coming from the thick brush. He withdrew so that he might better dispatch what was obviously a large snake. But the brush was so thick, that Milton decided he probably didn't want the berries as much as the snake did. Nor did he want the snake to think him greedy.

Just as Milton abandoned the hissing bush, he saw Harold working his way toward it. Milton immediately warned his friend of the danger that lurked within, but Harold, while a nice guy, just was not the type of person who liked other people telling him what to do. With sarcasm in his voice, he told Milton that *he* wasn't scared of snakes "like some people I know."

Milton again tried to warn Harold that he thought a snake was in the thick briers, but Harold only muttered something under his breath—something about "scaredy cats," and pushed fearlessly into the bush, reaching down for an especially large cluster of berries. There followed a loud hiss, a louder shout, and a flying Harold.

Coiled at the base of the vine was a large and obviously ornery cotton-mouth moccasin. It was angry and it could have been heard from 100 feet away. But the boys faced the challenge and quickly made of this poisonous snake another "good snake."

But the cotton-mouth did not go quietly; he had bitten Harold on the fleshy part of his right hand between his thumb and fore-finger. Harold was worried, and though Milton tried to comfort him, he, too, was worried. Milton suggested that he cut the area and suck the blood and venom from the wound, the way he had seen it done in the movies. He used his pocket knife in an attempt to cut slits in Harold's hand, but Harold wouldn't hold still long enough for an incision to be made. Finally, Milton wrapped Harold's hand in an old cloth, and they walked the two miles to Harold's house.

On the way, Harold remained calm. He walked into the house and told his parents he had been bitten by a snake. His parents showed none of their son's calmness. They rushed him to a doctor in Tuscumbia; his hand was now twice its normal size.

But, in two weeks, Harold was back helping Milton pick berries, now a veteran snake-bite victim, and a much more cautious one.

Milton and Harold, having learned that a hissing bush is one to walk away from, took their berries to Mr. White, who immediately placed an order for twenty more gallons. And under his breath he asked the boys to please not mention to anyone that he was making wine. The boys were puzzled by his request for secrecy, figuring that perhaps his wife didn't approve of his hobby and that women were funny that way.

In any event, blackberry picking became a summer sport, with Milton enjoying the adventure of dodging snakes and the encounters with wasps in hidden nests. Milton learned, that when it comes right down to it, there is very little difference between hunting berries and hunting snakes—where you find one, you are likely to find the other. He was never without his sturdy, six-foot-long, snake-dispatching stick. For a time he kept count of the snakes he had killed by notching the stick for each kill. Eventually, the stick was made as much of notches as it was of wood.

Chapter 20
A Night to Remember

When Milton was in the seventh grade at Cherokee Vocational High School, he met Billy, who lived in the mountains southwest of Cherokee. Billy had often asked Milton to spend the night with him.

Milton was reluctant to accept because he was afraid he would then have to ask Billy to spend some time at his house, where there wasn't enough room for an overnight guest. Milton held out as long as he could, but eventually gave in to Billy's persistence. His mother approved and gave him advice on how to behave when visiting another family. Her most important point was that he not do anything that would reflect poorly on his family name.

That day at school, Milton was excited that he would be having a new adventure, and looked forward to the ten-mile school bus ride to Billy's home. Billy and Milton got off the bus at a mail box back in the hills. A narrow trail led into the woods. After walking about 15 minutes through tall pine trees, they came to Billy's house. It was a large, three-room log cabin with a kitchen (serving as a combination living and dining room) and two bedrooms. There was no indoor plumbing; a path led to an outhouse at the rear of the cabin and another path led to a spring bubbling from the base of a cliff.

Billy introduced Milton to his parents and his two sisters. They were friendly people, and their conversation was sprinkled with plenty of "this heres" and "that theres," "we uns," "ain'ts" and other "hill talk." But Milton was used to being around mountain folk and found nothing objectionable in their speech.

Before dinner, Milton helped Billy with his chores. They carried several buckets of water from the spring, slopped the hogs, chopped wood and carried it to the house, and fed the mules and cattle. After their chores, they sat down to a supper of turnip greens, salt pork, and corn bread. Everything was delicious. Milton had eaten only a sandwich for lunch, but it didn't matter—he was hungry all the time.

After supper, the boys did their math homework by kerosene lamp. When they had finished, they listened to stories about "city slickers who thought they knew everything about everything," told by Billy's family. Milton briefly wondered whether they considered him a "city slicker" and were telling the stories to embarrass him. The entire family would laugh after each story. One of Billy's sisters had a laugh that reminded Milton of the braying of a mule. Though Milton didn't find many of the stories funny, he laughed to be polite. He was growing uncomfortable and was glad when Billy's mother said it was time for bed.

Milton had been wondering where he was to sleep. Billy led him into a bedroom and said they would be sleeping here. So the two boys stripped down to the underpants and got in bed. Then, to Milton's amazement, Billy's two sisters climbed into bed with them. Milton was so embarrassed that he was afraid to move. The bed was obviously crowded, and the room was very cold. Milton lay there, sandwiched between the two girls, and utterly afraid to move. Soon, all were asleep—but Milton.

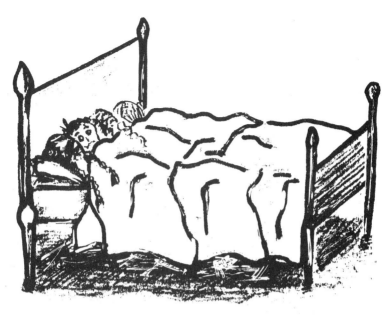

He must have lain awake for two or three hours. Everyone was snoring. Suddenly, Milton heard a loud noise under the floor of the bedroom. There was a lot squealing and grunting, and something bumped against the floor.   Milton sat upright in bed and woke one of the sisters sleeping next to him. He whispered, "What's that noise?" She sleepily replied, "Go back to sleep. That's only the hogs—their pen is under the house." She turned and went back to sleep. Milton, too, eventually drifted off to sleep until all four were shaken awake by Billy's mother, announcing that breakfast was ready. The boys and girls dressed and went to the kitchen where they washed up at a basin on a bench. Each used the same water and the same towel.

Billy's mother asked Milton if he had slept well, and Milton politely answered yes. There was nothing to be gained from telling the truth, he reasoned.

Breakfast consisted of beans, cornbread, and milk. Milton felt embarrassed about having beans and cornbread for breakfast. It was well known in the South that only the poorest people ate beans and cornbread for breakfast. He made a secret promise to himself not to tell anyone how poor Billy's family was. After all, Billy was a good friend. And he was also too embarrassed to tell anyone that he had slept with two girls who snored loudly and who, as the night grew colder, had snuggled up to him.

At school that day, it was hard for Milton to stay awake, but he sure was looking forward to returning to his own home—and his own bed—for the night. After that night at Billy's, Milton learned to appreciate his own home more and came to realize that his family was not as poor as he sometimes thought it was.

Chapter 21
Milton Goes to the State Fair

It was autumn once again, always welcome after a scorching Alabama summer. Milton had hoed cotton and corn all summer long, and he had been looking forward to the Alabama State Fair for months. He would be going with his cousin Charles to the fair grounds in Florence. He had worked hard all year to earn money for his school clothes and, from this amount, he had set aside six dollars for the fair. Bus fare to Florence was twenty cents and rides costs ten to twenty cents.

When Milton and Charles arrived at the fair grounds, several of their pals from Valdosta were already waiting for them at the entrance. Milton was 14 and full of energy. He had been looking forward to the cotton candy for quite a while, so that came first, but, thereafter, it was one ride after another. After a while, they began playing games along the midway. Some of the boys were trying to toss rings over bottles to win a teddy bear, but Milton went right to the shooting game, where .22 calibre rifles were tied to the counter.

Milton was considered a good shot by all those who had hunted with him. After all, couldn't he drop an evasive grey squirrel with one shot to the eye?

Milton paid the quarter for five shots. The object was to hit a small, red star in a target about 25 feet from the counter. If he hit the star he would get five dollars, about two days worth of work on the farm. But, as Milton prepared to shoot, it occurred to him that he had never seen anyone win at the shooting gallery. But he trusted his aim. His friends watched; they, too, wanted to shoot but were afraid that they would look bad. It looked so easy that Milton was already considering what he would do with the five dollars.

He aimed carefully, and his first shot took out most of the red star. He had hit it dead-center! "This is too easy," Milton thought. The next four shots also hit dead-center. He was bursting with pride; five bulls-eyes with his friends watching.

The gallery attendant retrieved the target and, placing his finger nails in the rear of the hole, pushed forward a bit of the red from the star and said, "Too bad. You didn't get all the red." Milton and friends made it known they weren't at all pleased by this trickery. But Milton did not want to make a scene, despite the attendant's practiced deception.

Later, Milton and Charles were walking the grounds when an attendant from another booth called to them. He tried to talk the boys into playing his game, which consisted of placing a dollar on a number. The attendant would then draw a number from a box, and if the numbers matched, the player received two dollars. Though the cousins said they weren't interested in playing, the man persisted, finally saying, "Boys, how about helping me out. Place a dollar on the table and we'll play for fun, just to show you how it's done." Milton, being an accommodating fellow, decided to help the poor man out.

Milton placed his dollar on the table and the man drew a number. Grabbing Milton's dollar, he said, "You lost, kid. Beat it." Milton couldn't believe it. He angrily told the attendant, "Give me my money back," using the gruffest voice a 14-year-old could manage. Unintimidated, the man again told him to beat it. Milton grew angrier and placed his hand inside his loose shirt near his belt. Sounding as menacing as he could, he said, "Give me my money now." The man asked what Milton had inside his shirt. Milton told the man that if he didn't return Milton's money, he would find out "pretty darn quick." "Darn" was the only "bad word" that Milton allowed himself to use, and then only when infuriated.

The bluff worked. The attendant was suddenly apologetic and fearful. He gave Milton his dollar, and said he had intended to return it all the time—that he was just playing games with Milton. He then retreated to the back of the booth as quickly as he could. Milton and Charles decided it was high time to catch the bus back to Tuscumbia and walk the mile home.

Chapter 22
The Big Fish Story

Next to his grandfather, Milton's Uncle Addison was the biggest inspiration to him. Uncle Addison grew up at Underwood Mountain, back in the woods near the base of a knoll on Smith Creek. He was born and reared in a log cabin divided into two sections, with a spring flowing in between. He spent his youth helping his father and brother farm.

Each winter, Addison and his brother spent much time hunting and trapping. They hunted squirrels and rabbits and trapped fox, raccoon, opossum and, sometimes, skunks. Uncle Addison would often tell Milton stories about his outdoor experiences as a young boy, and in that way was Milton's inspiration. His uncle had been able to purchase most of his clothing from the money he made selling the pelts of animals he had trapped. One such item—one in which he took particular pride—was a small, single-shot Steven's .22 calibre rifle. He kept this little rifle for twenty years; it was a symbol of his youthful experiences.

Milton didn't own a rifle at that time and, one day, asked his Uncle Addison if he might borrow his prized rifle for the day. His uncle agreed, but warned him to be very careful and to use only low-powered ammunition. Milton certainly agreed to Uncle Addison's reasonable terms, and on a warm July day, walked the two miles to Bear Creek with the rifle in hand.

Milton planned to "go fishing" with the rifle. He had planned to wade in the shallow backwaters of Bear Creek and shoot some of the large carp or buffalo fish that fed there. Some of those fish were more than three-feet long. They were a bit bony, but still quite edible.

Milton started slowly wading through the slough, alert for water moccasins and fish. He spotted several fish about fifty-feet away. The water was about eighteen-inches deep with a firm, muddy bottom. As Milton waded toward the feeding fish, a large water moccasin swam by, leaving a wake. Normally, Milton would have shot the snake, but he was concerned the shot would spook the fish.

As he approached the fish, he spotted a large one, perhaps forty-two inches long, preoccupied with feeding. He waded as near as he could to the monster, but it became alarmed and began swimming toward deeper waters. Milton aimed for the gills of the fish and fired. Blood spurted from the carp, which increased its speed in its mad dash toward deeper waters. Excited now, Milton followed the wounded fish and struck it over the head with his uncle's prized rifle. The bolt fell from the rifle and soon disappeared in the muddy bottom. After cracking the carp two or three times over the head, the carp was still alive and again dashing for deeper waters, trailing blood.

It was hard to say which was in worse shape: the rifle or the fish. The stock of the Stevens was cracked badly and, of course, the bolt was gone. Milton sat in the muddy water and began the search for the bolt. No luck! What would he tell his uncle? The only thing he could think of was that he had forgotten and used a more powerful shell than his uncle had recommended.

He then began rubbing the right side of his face with the rifle until his face was scratched and bleeding. He would tell his uncle that the rifle had blown up in his face, thereby hoping to gain some sympathy.

Needless to say, it was very difficult for Milton to return his uncle's once proud rifle in that condition. He attempted to explain what had happened, though it really bothered him to lie to his uncle, but Addison didn't seem all that angry.

Instead, Addison said he was sorry Milton had been hurt. Years later, he told Milton, "Who did you think you were fooling with that rifle story?" He had thought that perhaps Milton had been in a fight and had hit that person over the head with the rifle. However, he always remained a good friend and a great uncle to Milton until his death years later. Shortly after the fish incident, Milton was able to purchase his own .22, and with it share many exciting hours hunting squirrel with his beloved—and forgiving—Uncle Addison.

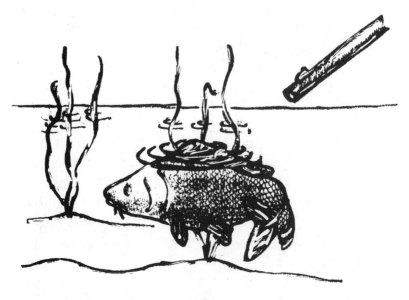

Chapter 23
Milton Goes Frog Hunting

As much as Milton and his friends enjoyed hunting squirrel, rabbit, and quail, they probably enjoyed dining on them more. But, because there were so many hunters in the area, game was often evasive and in short supply.

For this reason, an article Milton read in the Tri-Cities Daily caught his attention. The article told of restaurants in the North serving, of all things, frog legs. He had heard that some people thought they were delicious, particularly when fried like chicken. He had also heard that when fried. the legs actually jumped in the skillet. That was something he had to see. He knew where there were hundreds of plump-legged bull frogs along Bear Creek, and if they tasted as good as fried chicken, well, that was enough to motivate Milton.

Milton knew that the best time to hunt frogs was at night; the darker the night, the better the hunting. So, one particularly dark night, Milton and his friend Harold Olive loaded their old leaky boat with a flashlight, a kerosene lantern, a .12 gauge shotgun, and a frog gig attached to a ten-foot pole.

They paddled the boat to the far shore of Bear Creek and entered a slough of backwater that was no more than a foot deep in many places. Willow trees, with their branches drooping into the water, grew along the slough. During the day, this area was known as snake-infested. Milton dearly hoped that the many large snakes slept at night. Before the night was out, he would have his answer.

As the boys paddled and poled the boat through the shallow water, they could see ripples in the water as snakes swam away from the boat. Milton's next-best hope was that maybe these snakes were on their way home to sleep. In the glare of their flashlight, they could see the occasional reflection of frog and snake eyes.

The deep bellowing of the bull frogs filled the night and raised the boys' expectations of a successful hunt. The boys paddled toward the sound of the loudest bellows, reasoning that from large frogs come loud bellows. The boys imagined them to be like grand-daddy frogs: big with large legs.

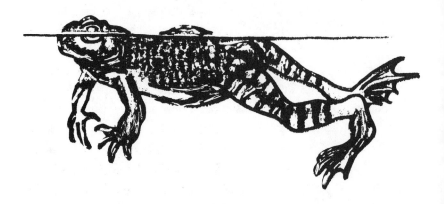

Their first attempts at spearing the bigger frogs were successful. But they had to take time to bail out their old wooden boat that took on water seemingly like a bathtub. And on one of the occasions, the boat drifted under a large willow branch, and a large cotton-mouth moccasin dropped into the center of the boat. It seemed to the boys in their mild state of shock that the moccasin was at least eight-feet long. Actually, moccasins never grow to that length, but fear has a way of exaggerating reality.

The boys couldn't jump from the boat fast enough. Harold had the presence of mind to grab the 12 gauge and blast the snake into pieces. Not present in his mind, however, was that he was also blasting a hole four-inches in diameter in the boat, which needed no assistance in taking on water.

There was little they could do at that point but bail as quickly as they could, the bucket filled with bloody water and pieces of squirming snake. They finally managed to plug the hole with an old shirt and were able to bail out the remainder of the water and re-enter the boat. After this unforgettable experience, the courageous lads decided to give the frogs "a break for the night." Their boat was small enough as it was without having to accommodate a cotton-mouth moccasin of unknown dimensions.

While paddling back to shore, they spotted several snakes swimming in front of the boat. It finally occurred to Milton that his hope that snakes sleep at night was nothing more than a hope, and that frog-hunting at night was a lousy idea because there seemed to be more snakes than frogs in the slough.

However, as frightening as the experience was, it did not deter Milton from continuing his night-time quest for frogs. He just became more cautious, doing his hunting from the shore. And the story about frog legs jumping in the skillet when being fried was never observed to be true by Milton.

Chapter 24
The Swimming Hole

The dog days of August were upon us again, reducing life—both human and animal—to a crawl. And no one disliked the heat of August more than Milton. His house would get as hot as an oven, even with all the windows open and the family's one electric fan turned on "high."

One such day Milton decided to spend at Bear Creek, fishing, swimming, and just loafing around. He rose before daylight and ate breakfast with his grandfather. Then, with the sun just breaking the eastern horizon, he walked the two miles along the railroad tracks to Bear Creek. He was already sweating, despite wearing only a pair of bib overalls and an old straw hat to protect him against the merciless Alabama sun. If it is this hot at dawn, he thought, what will it be like at noon? He would later learn that at noon it was 110 degrees with humidity at 90 percent: one miserable day.

Milton found the shadiest spot he could and began fishing. He fished only with a hook, line, and lead weight, which he carried in his pocket. Using his pocket knife, he cut a small pole, which he attached his line to. He was normally a patient fisherman, willing to sit for hours waiting for the fish to bite. But the air was dead and the heat oppressive. When he had no bites in the first hour, he decided that even the fish were too lazy to eat.

So he decided he'd go swimming —always a sure way to beat the heat. He walked back to the railroad tracks and over the trestle high above the creek. When he was about two-thirds of the way across, he happened to look over his shoulder and saw what is now called "his worst nightmare." A train was closing fast, but he had been so preoccupied with the oppressive heat that he had never given a thought to whether a train might be coming.

Milton was certain that, whatever he did, it had better be quick. He quickly determined that he couldn't outrun the train, which left only the options of either diving from the trestle or climbing over its edge until the train passed. He sensed that the trestle was just too high for him to dive from, so he climbed over the edge, and held on to an undergirding while the train passed.

Unfortunately, the train was a long freight, and its vibrations almost caused him to lose his grip. But he held onto the beam for dear life; he was covered with creosote that was seeping from the wood because of the intense heat.

When the train had passed, Milton—shaken but otherwise well—climbed back onto the trestle and finished crossing the creek. At the end of the trestle there was a path leading through the thick brush to a slough, where water had backed up, forming a swimming area. Milton and his pals often swam here. This was one of two main swimming holes on the creek.

The swimming hole Milton had chosen was safest because it had no drop-offs or deep holes. The bottom was a combination of clay and sand, and the water was rarely muddy, but Milton couldn't remember when the water had been so clear that he could see the bottom. The swimming hole was about two hundred feet wide and was very shallow. There was only one small area too deep to wade across.

At the swimming hole, he got out of his sticky, creosote-covered overalls and tried to scrub the creosote from them using sand and dirt from the slough bottom. This helped some, but creosote never really comes out, so it was just one more stain on Milton's already considerably stained overalls that he would have to live with.

He hung his overalls on a tree limb to dry and jumped

into the water. The water felt cold compared with the air. Milton lay on the bottom with about two feet of water separating him from the oppressive sun. The water felt so refreshing that he played in the swimming hole for several hours, and his face was turning a darker brown than he was used to. So he decided to again try his luck at fishing. His overalls were sure to have dried by now.

Just as Milton was walking from the water, he heard an approaching automobile. Wearing only the clothing he was born with, he hurried back into the water for cover. Back then, few boys would wear swimming suits.

No sooner had he had made it back into the water, when, not one, but two cars pulled up. And each car was packed with females, no doubt also seeking relief from the heat. Needless to say, their arrival ruined his fishing plans; there was no way he could get to his overalls without being seen in the altogether.

The women getting out of the cars were variously shaped: skinny, fat, plump going on fat, and the in-between. The timid among them tested the water with their toes before venturing in. Others entered the water gracefully like beauty queens, while the rest waddled into the water as best they could. Milton backed off until he was in water five-feet deep. The girls seemed to be looking at Milton as if to say, "What are you doing here, and what are you staring at?" To say the least, he was very uncomfortable.

Three hours later, the women were still splashing about in the swimming hole, and Milton had burned that much browner. They had included him in their games of chase and beach-ball punching. Finally, the women left the water, and Milton began feeling much better about his chances of avoiding embarrassment. But to his dismay, they had left only to have a snack along the bank. Milton, by this time, was starved, burned, and tired—though not necessarily in that order. One of the girls yelled for Milton to come out and have a sandwich and a cold drink with them, not realizing, or perhaps realizing only too well, that Milton was naked. He was so hungry that, for the briefest moment, he considered walking out in his birthday suit. But, instead, he lied: he yelled back that he wasn't hungry.

After the women had eaten their sandwiches and drunk their sodas, they returned to the water and resumed their play. Milton decided he had had enough: clothes or not he was going to leave the water and walk home. Just as he started walking to the shore, he heard the approach of another car. Uttering a moan (which perhaps included a "darn"), he returned to the deeper water. But Milton knew the people in the car. It was Mr. Walker, his wife, daughter, and young son. Milton had a crush on the young daughter and didn't want to be embarrassed any more than he already had been.

The family entered the water and waded out to Milton and began talking with him. Milton was embarrassed, but he knew they couldn't see beneath the water and resigned himself to making the best of a bad situation. Soon, he was playing and showing off in front of Mr. Walker's daughter. Mr. Walker would throw a bottle, and Milton would dive after it.

Finally, the group of women left the water and drove away. But the Walkers remained for another half-hour. As they were leaving, Mr. Walker asked Milton if he wanted a ride home. At this time, Milton quietly explained his situation to Mr. Walker, who had a good laugh. He got Milton's overalls and, wading back, brought them to him. Milton dressed underwater, and returned to shore.

The sun was so hot that it soon re-dried his overalls. He sat and had an R.C. Cola with the Walkers, and accepted their offer of a ride home. This was a day Milton never forgot. He began wearing a pair of cutoff overalls when he went swimming. He was not as comfortable, but never again was he as embarrassed as he was on that hot August day.

Chapter 25
The Alligator

On hot summer days, Milton and his friends would often walk the two miles to Bear Creek to swim and just to have a good time. Often, they would take a watermelon with them and place it in one of the cold springs flowing into the creek. In addition to making for excellent refreshment, afterwards, the watermelon could be used in a melon-rind fight.

On one particular day, Milton was the first to dive from the old bridge foundation. He resurfaced about thirty feet from the shore. Looking to the far shore, he saw what appeared to be a log about eight-feet long floating next to the bank. And then he saw it move. Milton almost certainly swam back to the shore in record time. After he caught his breath, he yelled to his companions that there was an allegator in the creek. No one believed him.

Apparently, he was the only one to see it. After all, alligators aren't found in North Alabama because the winters are too cold.

But Milton was certain he had seen an alligator, regardless of what the others thought. For the rest of the day, he sunned himself on the old bridge foundation instead of swimming with his friends. For Milton, this was most unusual behavior because he enjoyed the water so much.

About a week later, Milton was down on the creek by

himself. He was planning to fish upstream from where he usually swam. To get to his favorite fishing hole, he had to walk around a small slough. In the process, he almost stepped on an alligator that was more than six-feet long. Luckily, it was dead. Needless to say, Milton was scared half to death. Probing the carcass with a stick satisfied him that the gator was, indeed, dead. It had been shot in the head several times.

Milton couldn't help wondering how an alligator happened to be in Bear Creek. No one had ever heard of an alligator that far north. In asking around Valdosta, he learned that two men had observed the alligator from a boat as it slept on the creek bank. The men had been visiting their whiskey still. They said they shot the gator several times in the head with a small-calibre rifle and towed it upstream to their camp. They said that, once they had returned to their camp, the gator, which they thought was dead, killed two of their hounds before dying of its wounds. They had then thrown the carcass back into the creek and, apparently, it had drifted down the creek to the slough.

Later, Milton learned that his friend Jimmy, the grandson of the owner of the Lily Pond general store, had bought the alligator in Florida while on vacation. He kept his "pet" in a wash tub at the rear of the store until it had grown too large. He then threw it into Lily Pond behind the store.

A few years later, when the pond had gone dry, Jimmy had recaptured the alligator—now much larger—and had taken it to Bear Creek. It had probably survived the colder winters by living in underwater caves along the creek. Jimmy's grandfather told Milton that it saddened him that the alligator had been killed after surviving so long under such harsh conditions.

After his alligator experience, Milton always checked

carefully before swimming in Bear Creek. He had learned to deal with snakes, but alligators were a different story. Milton had nothing against sharing, but sharing a swimming hole with an alligator was asking too much of anyone.

Chapter 26
Milton's First Fishing Rod

During the Depression, fishing was more than a sport: it was a way of eating and of surviving. And it also provided a much-needed distraction during those hard times. So, whenever possible, people fished.

One of the best times for fishing was in the early spring when the striped bass were spawning. Milton and his friends would hike the two miles to Bear Creek and spend the day fishing from the limestone formations on the bank. Worms were the bait of choice; they cost nothing other than the effort involved in digging them out. Sometimes, Milton would trap minnows and use them for bait, but, for bass, worms worked best.

On a Saturday in April, Milton was sitting on a limestone ledge catching an occasional striped bass. He was using a long hickory pole as a fishing rod, ten feet of line, a sinker, and a small, worm-baited hook. During such times, he often wondered whether worms had feelings. He truly hoped not because he had drowned hundreds of them, and fed many hundreds more to the fish population of North Alabama.

On his stringer, he had eight nice bass; not a bad start for so early in the morning. Some of those fishing along with Milton had modern rods and reels, but they weren't catching any more fish than Milton. The cost of new rods and reels was far beyond what Milton and some of his friends could afford. To compensate for their envy, they would make fun of the "city slickers" who owned the best rods and reels. But deep down, they would have loved to have the best equipment.

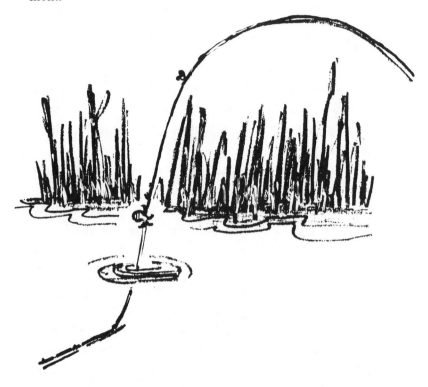

Milton knew it would be a long time before he could afford a new rod and reel, so it was important for him to out-fish those who had fancy equipment. And, using his old hickory rod, he usually did, but he couldn't help wondering how much better he would do with "city slicker" equipment.

Just then, Milton's pole bent as a fish took the bait and took off as far as it could with ten feet of twenty-pound test line. Milton jerked the pole to bring the fish in, and a large bass fell from his hook and back into the water. He still felt pressure on his line, and as he pulled it in, he found a red-and-white striped spoon tangled in his line. He pulled the spoon in, and saw that attached to the last bit of line was a Model 1920 Shakespeare Wonder Reel and Rod.

Surely, this was a dream come true—he finally had his new rod and reel and it hadn't cost him a penny. He took the rod and reel home and disassembled and oiled the reel mechanism. It was in perfect working condition. Milton was unable to learn the identity of the original owner, though it must be said he didn't tire himself out looking for him. He used that "miracle" rod and reel for many years and, in fact, it did prove much better than the hickory pole. He finally resolved that owning a "real" rod and reel was worth the risk of being called a "city slicker."

Chapter 27
The Rolling Store

During the Depression, few people owned car; they either walked or depended on those who did drive for transportation. Because of the many families living in rural areas, a few enterprising people operated "rolling stores." The stores-on-wheels had established routes and followed fairly accurate schedules. Consequently, people became very dependent on them.

Sometime in the late '30s, Milton remembered "borrowing" eggs from neighborhood hen houses to trade for penny candy. To the owners of the rolling stores, eggs were worth one-cent. If the owner of the store later found the eggs to be rotten, he would demand that they be replaced on his next trip.

With the advent of the rolling store, it wasn't long before hen houses throughout Valdosta were being raided for eggs to trade for candy. Nickel candy in those days, as Milton remember, gave you as much as a fifty-cent candy bar does today. When the eggs were in short-supply, the boys would go into the woods and dig sassafras roots, clean and tie them in bundles, and trade them for candy. The rolling stores also took chickens in trade. However, most of the boys were afraid of the consequences of stealing a neighbor's chicken or of the greater consequences of taking one from the parents, who kept a daily record of their numbers. In those days, livestock and vegetables were all that stood between families and poverty. Just about everyone raised a garden or had livestock of some sort. Milton and his friends may not have had nice clothes, but they always ate well.

When Milton was in the eighth grade, he was hired by a rolling store company in Lily Pond. His job was to load the two trucks each evening, six days a week. He had to work two hours each evening and drew about nine dollars and sixty cents a week, not much by today's standards but an invaluable source of income to Milton. After a year on the job, Milton asked for a raise to twelve dollars a week. The owner's wife agreed but her banker husband at first refused. It was hard work. Milton loaded heavy bags of livestock feed aboard the rolling store, as well as many other items, none of which seemed to be light. The only way he was able to get his raise was to threaten to quit. It was something of a bluff. He didn't really want to quit, and he knew that half the boys of Valdosta wanted his job. So he was relieved when the owner reluctantly agreed to his terms.

On some Saturdays, Milton would ride on the rolling store and help the driver-clerk. Saturday was always a busy day; some Saturdays they would sell more than a thousand dollars in goods. The driver was paid forty dollars a week plus a small commission on total sales. Milton received an extra four dollars a week for working on Saturdays. The day started at 6 AM, and he worked through to 6 or 7 PM. Milton's main Saturday job was to fill kerosene cans from the tank mounted at the rear of the rolling store. Many people still used kerosene lamps because the cost of wiring one's home for electricity was considered an unaffordable luxury.

The rolling store carried many snacks, such as candy,

cookies, sardines, bologna, cheese and crackers, and soft drinks. Small boxes of crackers were five cents.

The older folks seemed to have a preference for cheese and crackers. Sardines were five cents. For a total of fifteen cents, you could buy crackers, a can of sardines, and an R.C. Cola. When prices started going up, the driver would usually have a smart reply to those who complained. When poor people (especially black folks) complained, he would hold up a piece of cheese and tell them to smell it because a whiff was all that five cents could buy. However, if the person complaining about the price increase was old (and, especially, white) he would cut them a small slice of cheese or bologna and hand them a few loose crackers.

The rolling stores also accommodated special customers who ordered items the store didn't normally carry. The driver would take their orders and attempt to find it and deliver it a week later on his next scheduled visit. Milton remembered a Yankee (he spoke with an accent) who asked for a brand of cigarette not sold in the South. The driver couldn't understand why anyone would want one of those long cigarettes with a filter in one end. The driver told Milton that the filter would rob the cigarette of its flavor and that "filters would never catch on." For the most part, he sold only Lucky Strikes, Camels, and Chesterfields.

Milton marveled at how people so poor could smoke so many cigarettes. Everyone seemed to have a cigarette dangling from the corner of their mouth. Milton thought pipe-smokers had the right idea. The rum-maple tobacco mix that his grandfather smoked had a wonderful aroma. Milton once tried a pipe but found that he preferred the smoke under his nose rather than in his throat.

Milton had decided at an early age that he was going

to be a smoker. Of course, his mother, grandfather, and uncles refused to allow the younger members of the family to smoke. This made no sense to Milton because they all smoked. After all, even the stars in the movies (which Milton faithfully attended most Saturday nights) were always smoking. From the movies, he drew the conclusion that important people smoked.

Despite the warnings from his relatives, Milton started smoking at an early age, though his attempts were most unpleasant. He would roll corn husks, light the end, and attempt to smoke. Corn husks not only didn't taste good but they would burn his throat if he inhaled. He next experimented with a weed, known as rabbit tobacco. He would dry it and roll it in a page from a Sears catalogue. But it sure didn't taste very good. Perhaps, he thought, he was doing something wrong.

Next, he decided to chew tobacco. His good friend, Bennie Mitchell, always had a chew of either Mule, Days Work, or Beechnut in his mouth. Of course, Bennie was always spitting a lot, and spitting accurately, too. He could out-spit anyone Milton knew. One day he offered Milton a chew of Mule. Bennie cut off a small piece of the chewing tobacco and told Milton to chew on it and then let the tobacco lay in the corner of his mouth, telling him, "After a while, it will taste good." Milton walked home with the tobacco in his mouth, following Bennie's advice and spitting often. When he got home he was met by his Uncle Sam who wanted to know what was in Milton's mouth. Milton said there was nothing in his mouth, and he was telling the truth. Because as soon as his uncle had asked, Milton swallowed the tobacco.

Milton was sick for three weeks after swallowing that Mule tobacco. Even the thought of tobacco made him feel sick. He lost his appetite and some weight; for a time folks said he was looking like a skeleton, and Milton felt like one, too. He swore that he would never again chew tobacco. Unfortunately, Milton was weak when it came to making resolutions. One day Bennie told him that apple tobacco tasted better. Milton figured that Bennie must be right. After all, he was an expert tobacco-chewer and it didn't make him sick. Milton stuffed the apple tobacco in his mouth and within five minutes, he was again vomiting.

Milton finally determined that chewing tobacco was not for him. But he had great respect for Bennie, figuring a fellow must really be tough to be able to chew tobacco as easily as Bennie did.

Milton was embarrassed that he couldn't handle chewing tobacco and thought that, maybe, he could smoke it without becoming sick. So he and a cousin went to Tuscumbia where they bought cigars for ten cents. Returning home, they walked into a corn field and lit up. Well, to make a long story short, Milton filled his lungs with cigar smoke and thought he was going to die. He became so sick, he almost wished he would die and be out of his misery. However, this episode did cure Milton of any desire for tobacco for the rest of his life.

Milton worked in the rolling-store warehouse part-time   and on the store Saturdays until he finally enlisted in the Air Force and left North Alabama for good. But the memories of his youth there are as pleasant to him as the aroma of his grandfather's rum-maple pipe. The simple times proved to be the best of times.

Chapter 28
Bear Creek Cave

When Milton was growing up, he took advantage of every opportunity to explore the hills and hollows of North Alabama. His greatest interest was in the exploration of caves. One cave that Milton remembers, and very much desires to return to, is a cave on Bear Creek near the Tennessee River.

The entrance to this cave consisted of a large overhanging cliff about fifty feet from the creek. This overhang provided an excellent site for camping. At the left side of the overhang was a twelve-foot drop into a large chamber that was about twenty-by-thirty feet. The only way into or out of the chamber was by ladder or rope. When he first discovered there was a cave by the overhang, Milton went looking for something to help get him down into the chamber. He cut down a cedar tree, about fifteen-feet long, with lots of limbs that could serve like the rungs of a ladder.

Once down the shaft, he saw that the cave was dry and somewhat dusty. As he moved into the cave, he lit several candles, which he carried in his pack for this purpose, and stuck them on ledges throughout the main chamber of the cave. Then, taking his flashlight and hatchet, he explored one of the small passageways leading from the main chamber. He followed one passageway for about fifty feet, until it narrowed to about five feet high and six feet wide.

The tunnel ultimately led to an oval-shaped hole with a large rock supported over a three-by-three foot entrance by two large and very old red-cedar posts. The cedar posts were so old that only the red core remained. Milton touched the edge of one post, and the rotten wood crumbled away, but he was careful not to brush against the supporting posts. Entering the small chamber was a frightening experience. But being young and inexperienced, Milton was of the mind that bad things happened only to others. After all, wasn't he still alive?

The chamber that he entered was approximately four-feet high and six-feet deep. To his amazement, he found that the rear wall of the chamber was closed with flat stones mortared together. He couldn't figure out what a mortared wall was doing at the rear of a deep, underground cave.

He attempted to break through the wall with his hatchet, but made no progress. Whoever had cemented the wall—and it appeared to have been done a very long time ago—had done an excellent job. In later years, Milton read that Indians often buried their dead and sealed the chamber with mortar made from mussel shells, ground to a fine consistency and mixed with animal blood. This not only made for strong mortar, but for mortar that grew stronger with age.

As he lay on the floor of the chamber attempting to hack his way through the wall, Milton happened to shine his flashlight on the ceiling. He saw what appeared to be several bones protruding through the limestone. The bones, yellowed with age, crumbled when he touched them. He never found out what kind of bones they were, but they appeared to be human, either leg or arm bones. If the darkened cave seemed spooky before, it seemed positively haunted now, and Milton decided to get out. He could look back to the main chamber and see shadows cast by his candles dancing on the cave walls. It was, indeed, time to leave.

Despite his persistent efforts, Milton was never able to find anyone who knew anything about the mortared wall or what might lie behind it. Just as unfortunately, Milton was never able to return to the cave. But its wonder has never left him. Was it an Indian burial chamber? What was the meaning of the large rock propped up by cedar logs over the entrance? Might there have been a buried treasure behind the wall? Or, more simply, perhaps someone in the distant past just blocked the tunnel to prevent someone from entering a dangerous area. Perhaps, someday, Milton will have the answer to his questions.

Chapter 29
Moo Cave

There was once a comic strip titled "Alley Oop." The characters were from prehistoric times. Influenced by that comic strip, Milton and his pals named a cave, located in the face of a two-hundred-foot cliff, above the Tennessee River, Moo Cave.

The cave was named Moo because it was similar to the cave lived in by the characters in Alley Oop. Moo Cave was a dream for Milton and his buddies. It was really a series of caves along a ledge about one hundred and twenty feet above the river. Some of the caves were almost like rooms or lean-tos. The entrances were large and extended fifteen to twenty feet back into the face of the cliff.

The cave the boys liked most was "Moo," which was a large recess in the face of the cliff having a large column of limestone supporting the front overhang. This section was approximately forty-feet long and ten- to twenty-feet deep.

Milton and his friends would often camp on the cliff ledge and look out over the river, about one-hundred yards away. On the face of the cliff and at its base, large trees grew in profusion. In the summer, these trees seemed to the boys like a jungle; large, wild grapevines hung from many of the trees. Often, the boys would cut the vines off at their base and swing out over the cliff. This was a real thrill, though, as Milton now recognizes, not the smartest thing he has done. It never occurred to the boys that a vine might break or tear loose from its tree, sending them forty feet straight down. But youth is invulnerable, and, to the best of Milton's knowledge, no one ever fell.

Inside Moo cave there was a tunnel that stretched back for about forty feet. The ceiling was seven- to ten-feet high and was always covered with spiders, big, long-legged ones. No matter how often Milton saw them, he could never quite feel comfortable in their presence. At the rear of this tunnel, there had once been a cave-in, and the tunnel was blocked except for a hole about fifteen-inches high, apparently the home of some small animal.

Milton was always tempted to dig out the caved-in area to see what might lie beyond it. But he could get no one to help him, and he wasn't about to work back in that cave alone. The boys probably thought that because it was Milton's idea, it wasn't a very good one. They remembered the time

Milton convinced them that they could get a fox to leave its den by filling the den with water. After emptying what seemed like half the creek down that hole, the fox was still there, and Milton's pals left in disgust. After that disaster, no one wanted to have anything to do with one of Milton's schemes.

Another interesting aspect of Moo cave was a small tunnel located near the main entrance. This small tunnel was somewhat a test of bravery. It was barely large enough for the boys to crawl through to get to the main tunnel. The bravery came in the fact that, once in the tunnel, there was no way to turn back, or, in some spots, even to back up.

When he was much older, Milton heard that a boy had entered this tunnel at its narrowest point and was unable to get through. As he started to back out, his heavy jacket bunched up and he became struck. He was trapped for more than eight hours until a small man was able to reach him and cut his jacket, piece by piece, until the boy was able to back out. According to the story Milton had heard, that was the last cave the boy would enter, and he was haunted by nightmares for a long time after the incident.

Milton certainly was no stranger to Moo cave during his teens. He would camp over with friends or just visit and imagine that he was an Indian living in a cave.

When Milton was 13, his scout troop made a field-trip to Moo cave, cooked a meal, and dug up sections of the floor looking for Indian relics. They found several stone beads, pieces of clay pottery, and flint chips. But the yield was hardly worth the effort. Had they known the proper way to excavate the area, their chances of finding something really worthwhile would have been much greater.

One weekend, Milton and several friends went camping at Moo cave. They took very little food; they were going to "Indian-it" for two days, or live off the land as the Chickasaw Indians did in North Alabama. From the surrounding area, Milton returned with apples, pears, hickory nuts, and black walnuts. One of the boys took his .410 shotgun on the trip and planned to shoot wild game for supper. True to his word, he returned with a rabbit, but that rabbit must have been the sickest rabbit in Alabama, if taste was any indication. Had the hunter shot an old rubber tire, they would have dined as well. But Milton's fruit and nuts, washed down with cold spring water, saved the meal.

Their second day of camping was much better. One of their friends came down to the cave to spend the night with them, bringing with him a case of Vienna sausages. Needless to say, he was welcomed with open arms. Though he was never question about how he got them, he later explained that he "found" them outside the grocery warehouse where he worked. The expression for that night was not "Indian-it," but "finders keepers; losers weepers." And after the rabbit stew, who could blame them?

Milton made countless trips to Moo cave, alone or with friends during his teen years, and, later, with his family. During his last visit, it was apparent that Moo was no longer the attraction in once was, if one were to judge from the lack of paths to the cave.

These days, Milton is a bit saddened that today's teens no longer seem to derive the same pleasure he did from the outdoors. Of course, when Milton was a teenager, there was no television, and most folks didn't even own a car. Perhaps Milton and his friends enjoyed their spare time so much because they had so little of it—everyone had to work so hard. In Milton's time, life was simpler but so very much more enjoyable. It was a time, perhaps never to be relived, when people relied on each other—and God's Green Earth—for companionship.

Chapter 30
Milton and the Boat

Milton hated to admit it, but he had one terrible temper, and often did things that he would later regret. Fortunately, his temper never got him into serious trouble; even most of his fights were more like wrestling matches. Once he had thrown an opponent (or been thrown) his anger usually left him. He was a good wrestler, though, and usually came out on top. He tried to avoid hitting anyone with his fists because it bothered him that he might hurt someone.

Milton certainly was not a bad boy but neither was he a saint. Like most boys in the valley, he was not above taking a watermelon or a cantaloupe from a neighbor's field, or, on occasion, cutting a sorghum cane to chew. But there was one time when his actions could have had serious consequences.

On the banks of Spring Creek, where Milton spent a lot of time hunting, hiking, and fishing, he would often pass a slough that backed up from the creek into a ditch. Once, while passing the slough, he saw that someone had chained and locked an old skiff to a tree. He couldn't understand why anyone would leave a boat in such an inaccessible location. Moreover, he'd never seen anyone using the boat. Over the next few days, it occurred to him that he might use the boat on Spring Creek without anyone noticing it. For weeks, he overcame that temptation, until he talked himself into believing that the owner had simply abandoned the boat. And, if that were the case, it would be a shame to see a boat locked to a tree and slowing rotting away.

Since Milton had strong feelings against stealing, he decided that he would only "borrow" the boat. Having resolved the problem of morals, Milton's only remaining problem was the large padlock securing the boat's chain to a large willow tree. Milton could use the hatchet that he always carried with him, but he was afraid the noise of metal on metal might draw unwanted attention. After all, he was only "borrowing" the boat. But, having grown up in the country, Milton knew that, just like there was more than one way to skin a cat, there was more than one way to bypass a lock.

Ten minutes later, Milton had picked the lock using a piece of wire he found lying on the bottom of the boat. He was proud of himself; he had never before attempted anything as complicated as picking a lock—it was almost too easy. He wondered if all locks were as easy to pick as this one had been, but was soon ashamed of having such thoughts, which were normally associated with stealing.

It was now time, as watchman of the boat, to try her out with a run down the creek to the Tennessee River. Using an old board for a paddle, Milton soon reached the river. The river was muddy and high; the current fast. Small trees and other debris were flowing past the boat. It was not the ideal time for further adventure, so he began to turn about and return the craft to the slough. Just then, he saw someone on the other side of the creek walking toward him. Afraid it might be the "real" owner of the boat, and that the owner might have a real revolver, Milton headed for the swift current of the Tennessee rather than risk a confrontation. What followed was a ride that was both thrilling and terrifying. Using the makeshift paddle, his control over the boat ranged from little to none. The boat began spinning and was bumped into the face of the high cliff that bordered the river. He bounced from the cliff into a small whirlpool, and the boat began filling with water. He stopped paddling and frantically began bailing the water out, but it was too late.

With the skiff sinking under him, Milton seemed to have no choice but to abandon ship—a tough decision for Milton because he was a poor swimmer. Just then, the swift current swept the boat past the cliffs and into a line of trees along the shore. Milton was soaked to the skin, but he managed to pull the boat ashore and empty the water from it. Staying in the shallows, he found another slough below Moo cave where he re-tied the boat. Of course, Milton had long since regretted his decision to "borrow" the skiff and was only too glad to take the much longer—but much drier and safer-route home.

Milton did not venture back to the boat for a week. When he finally summoned the courage to return, the boat was no longer where he had left it. His first reaction was anger that someone would steal "his" boat. After all that he'd been through, surely he should have been able to enjoy the skiff one more time.

Later, Milton was glad that the boat had been removed. For he learned that its owner was a mean character who had killed a man a few years earlier and who was suspected of making moonshine whiskey. Milton had no clear idea where this man might be, so he stayed away from any place he even thought the man might be. That old, rotten boat was the last thing that 14-year-old Milton ever stole. Of course, hunting squirrels out of season and trapping fish with illegal wire-baskets was still okay.

Chapter 31
The Peanut Incident

When Milton was 13, his grandfather decided to raise an acre of peanuts. Naturally, Milton was excited, not only because he loved nuts, but because peanut shells were so easy to open, unlike hickory nuts, wild pecans, and black walnuts. He wouldn't need a rock or his teeth to open those peanuts. He could fill his pockets in the morning and have a snack anytime he wanted.

The peanuts came up on schedule, and Milton helped his grandfather hoe the weeds and Johnson grass from around the crop. Those were long hours in the hot Alabama sun, the red soil all but baking his bare feet. But he didn't complain; the peanuts would be his reward.

When the peanuts matured in late summer, Milton's grandfather dug them up and stacked the vines around posts throughout the field. This allowed the peanuts to dry, which took about a month. The crop would then be gathered in burlap bags for storage until the surplus could be sold. Needless to say, Milton could hardly wait for the peanuts to dry and have his dream come true—pockets full of peanuts. He was foolish enough to try a few before they dried and paid for his impatience with several bad stomach aches.

Word eventually got around Valdosta that Milton's grandfather had mounds of peanuts stacked out in the field, and this attracted many of the village's teenage boys. Milton patiently explained that his grandfather would give them plenty when the peanuts had dried.

But, boys being boys, some of Milton's friends didn't really believe him. They told Milton that if he were really their friend, he would share the peanuts and not keep them all for himself. So, loyal friend that he was, Milton led them to the peanut field and told them they could eat all they wanted on the spot, but that they weren't to take any of the nuts with them. Milton was not surprised when he later learned that some of his friends were a bit under the weather and remaining close to their out-houses.

One day, Milton's grandfather was talking with his friends at the general store when one of the men jokingly said that he had heard there was a good supply of peanuts stacked out in the Thompson field. The remark was overheard by a young man of questionable character, who told Milton's grandfather that he was going to go out some moonlit night and help himself to a bag of peanuts. Milton's grandfather replied that when the peanuts were dried and bagged he would be happy to give the man a bag, but that it would not be wise to attempt to steal any. The unscrupulous man accepted the challenge and said that peanuts taken by moonlight tasted better and that he would let Milton's grandfather know how good they were. Grandpa Thompson said nothing; he only stared at the young man.

During the days that followed, Milton noticed that his grandfather would go out and check on his peanuts on moonlit nights. One night, just before Milton went to bed, he heard two blasts from a shotgun. His grandfather later told him that he had been sitting in the shadow of a peanut stack waiting for the avowed thief to make good on his word. He told Milton he first saw the young man crossing a neighbor's field and climbing the barbed-wire fence that separated the farms. The young man, he said, was carrying a large burlap bag and began filling the bag with peanuts. His grandfather said he raised the shotgun and pointed it at the thief. Light from the moon reflected off the barrel of the shotgun and drew the young man's immediate attention. He dropped his bag and began running toward the fence. Milton's grandfather stood up and fired both barrels into the air over the young man's head. His grandfather said he had never seen a man make better time over a barbed-wire fence.

For several months, the young man in question avoided areas where he might run into "Mr. Sam" (as Milton's grandfather was known to his friends). The man later related to friends that he was never so scared as he was that night when he saw that shotgun, its barrel glistening in the moonlight, being leveled at him. He said he had torn his pants on the fence and had fallen several times in his wild flight, expecting at any moment to feel shotgun pellets rip through his body. It was not surprising that he advised those friends not to mess with Mr. Sam.

Incidentally, Milton's dream did come true. The crop finally dried, and he had all the peanuts he could possibly want.

Chapter 32
The Mules

In the early forties, times were hard beyond words in the South. Many of the black farmers in the Valdosta area couldn't afford to feed their mules in the winter, so they would turn them loose for the season to forage in the neighboring fields. This did nothing to endear them to the owners of those neighboring fields. Sometimes, the mules would come up to the barns of the neighboring farmers and compete for food with their mules and cattle. The farmers and their sons would shoot the stray mules with slingshots to discourage their boldness. Occasionally, one of those mules would be killed by a car on Highway 72.

Meanwhile, most of the local boys frequently went to Saturday matinees to watch Gene Autry, Tom Mix, Buck Jones, Johnny Mackbrown, Randolph Scott and many other Western heroes. For those under 12, the cost was only ten cents. The cost was twenty-five cents for those 12 or older. Many of Milton's friends remained eleven for an abnormally long time.

It was the dream of every boy back then to have his own horse and play cowboy. But times were so hard that a horse was out of the question. One day, while Milton was walking down into the valley where many of his friends lived, he was invited by one of the older boys to accompany him up the hill to a wooded area. He said he had something he wanted to show Milton.

In a grove of pine and oak, about a hundred yards from the nearest house, the older boys had built a club house. And to Milton's amazement, there were five mules in a fenced area the boys had constructed using saplings and boards. The mules were the poorest excuses for mules that Milton had ever seen. Underfed as they were, they were scrawny, ill-tempered, and ugly. But his friends were proud that they had been able to round up the strays and were looking forward to riding them in their games of cowboy.

Had the mules known what was in store for them, there would have been no reason for their orneriness. For the boys had cut a large stack of grass and "borrowed" several bales of hay and bags of corn from farmers on a moonlit night.

The disposition of the mules improved soon enough. Milton doubted they would have been able to drive the hungry creatures away from the food bins with a horse whip. So far, this was turning out to be "mule heaven."

Because none of the boys had saddles, they used burlap bags to cushion skinny backsides from the bony-backed mules. Everything was going along nicely until it soon became obvious that the mules were not used to being ridden. They were primarily used for pulling plows and wagons.

The next step for the boys was to put together makeshift bridles and fit them to the mules' mouths. So ornery were the mules that it required four boys using ropes to hold a mule for the fifth boy to mount. Once on the mule, and the ropes released, the rider was on his own, for better or worse—and it was usually worse. The mules would snort and buck in an attempt—usually successful—to throw the rider.

What was worse, the mules would bite and kick if given half a chance. So the boys were always very aware of where they were in relation to the mule. Once away from the food, the mules would turn and run back to the bin, often dumping their riders in the process. But the boys kept at it, and as spring neared, they were able to play a pretty decent game of cowboys, chasing each other through the woods and across the fields. Riding at night was especially fun because they could ride across fields without any real fear of being seen by the farmer.

On a cool March day, an old black man came looking for his mule and that of his brother. He told the boys that the mules had broken away at the onset of winter. But Milton's friends knew that it was far more likely that the man and his brother had released the mules to feed off the land. So the

146

boys said simply that they didn't know anything about the missing mules. The man said that he didn't know what he would do if he couldn't locate his mules. He said, "Boys, I've got to grow a crop so I can feed my family." But the boys continued to plead ignorance.

After a few days, with their conscience beginning to nag them, they decided to charge the mule owners for feeding the animals all winter, but they knew that the men probably didn't have the money. So they just turned the mules loose, thus bringing to an end the "Season of The Mules." After all, there was always next year....

Chapter 33
The Troop Train

During the dark days of World War II, Milton and a few of his friends were sitting on the porch of the Lily Pond general store. This porch had an overhang that kept it in perpetual shadow, and always cooler than the afternoon sun. Milton could frequently be found on that porch with a bottle of R.C. Cola in one hand and a moon pie in the other. It was a good place to kill time during the blistering Alabama summers. They were like a reviewing stand for the cars passing along the highway or the trains moving in front of the store. The hotter the day, the more crowded the reviewing stand.

Milton enjoyed his visit to the old general store in Lily Pond for several reasons: the store carried an impressive variety of goods, and he was always likely to run into someone he knew. A section of the store even protruded over the pond, which filled about five acres. Farmers watered their cattle and their teams from the pond; and Milton and his friends pulled more than their share of perch, carp, and catfish from its waters. Lilies flourished throughout the pond, hence the name Lily Pond.

The general store was of frame construction and was covered with pressed tin squares. Inside, a counter stretched along one entire side, with the merchandise on shelves behind the counter. Located in the center of the counter was an old cash register and a credit-slip rack.

In the back of the store was a large pot-bellied wood stove with chairs and benches surrounding it. It was here that the older men of the area would hold forth on the major issues of the day. At the time of our story, the issues that dominated conversation were Hitler, the Japanese, and Milton's generation going to the dogs. Their commentary would be punctuated with the spit of their chewing tobacco into—or, more often, around—one of several cans around the stove.

The small rear porch of the store extended over the pond. On the porch, the owner kept cooped chickens that he had taken on trade and a tank of kerosene for lamps. At the edge of the porch was an outhouse—a two-seater.

The left side of the general store was reserved for racks and shelves where clothing, shoes, and similar items could be bought. Feed for livestock was kept further back. The mixture of the different feeds—for cattle, horses, chickens, and hogs—combined to produce a different and, in its own way, wonderful smell, an aroma that Milton would find at no other place for the rest of his life. The smell of the wood floor, which daily was treated with oil before being swept, also contributed to the uniqueness of the Lily Pond general store. In short, that old store had a smell of its own: sweet, pungent, unique—a smell that is as secure in Milton's memory as anything he might have touched or done.

For Milton, through, the store's greatest attraction was the old parrot kept in a cage at the rear of the store. That parrot could out-cuss any sailor and whistled at every woman who came into the store.

One day, when Milton and his buddies were sitting on benches in the shaded porch of the general store, a troop train passed. There was nothing new about watching a troop train pass, but this one stopped and backed up until it was directly across the highway from the general store. The train was carrying Marines to a naval base for eventual transportation to the South Sea Islands, and ultimately, combat with the Japanese. The train also carried military police to prevent any reluctant Marine from going AWOL.

As usual, it was a hot summer day. After watching the train for a while, Milton noticed one of the Marines gesturing to him to cross the highway to the train, which Milton did. The Marine asked him if he would get him a Coke, which, back then, cost five cents. The Marine gave Milton a quarter and told him to keep the change. Milton was only to happily to oblige; as a matter of fact, he would have done the favor for nothing. Marines were his heroes; they were fighting for his country. When Milton returned with the Coke, other Marines put in their orders for Cokes, cookies, and candy.

The Marines kept handing money to Milton until both his pockets were full. Milton made so many trips back and forth from the train that he exhausted the store's supply of snacks. Even the guards were ordering refreshments. Milton made a lot of money for the store that day, so the owner gave him a few dollars for his efforts.

Sitting on a bench in the shade was a beautiful girl whose name was Maryellen. The granddaughter of the store owner, she had long blonde hair and carried herself with great dignity—a real southern belle. Milton hadn't been paying much attention to her. After all, she was older, and Milton had yet to figure out why there was a need for girls when there was so much hunting and fishing to be done. Besides, he was never going to marry. He was going to be an outdoorsman. But, while Milton hadn't noticed her, everyone on board the troop train had. They were calling out to her and waving. One of the Marines summoned Milton back to the train and gave him a note to give to the girl "with the long blonde hair." Milton returned with the note just as the train was pulling out.

Three-years later, the Marine who had given the note to Maryellen (his name was George) came back to Alabama and married her. The note had asked Maryellen to write to him while he was overseas. She did, and their romance blossomed.

Maryellen's father was a cotton farmer. After the wedding, Maryellen's father gave George a job on his farm. He was to be a working supervisor of the hired hands hoeing cotton. His job was to use his hoe to rid the cotton of weeds and space the cotton plants.

The work was hard in the intense heat of Alabama. George was from New Jersey and used to neither the heat nor the demanding physical labor. Nor could he distinguish between the cotton and the common morning-glory vine that grew everywhere in the South. His father-in-law finally decided in would be better to find George another job, which is how George became a postman. The last time Milton saw George, he was told that the couple had several children and that it was all his fault for delivering that fateful message on the day the troop train stopped.

Chapter 34
Milton's Grandfather

Milton's grandfather was named Samuel Walker Thompson. He was born in 1883 and he would tell stories of when he was young. After Milton had grown up and left home he wished that he would have listened to more of his grandfather's stories. Milton remembered some of his stories and among his favorites are these.

Tell Me a Big Lie

Sam had two cousins. One was John and the other Cletus. Cletus had a reputation for being lazy and often stretching the truth. John was a hard worker and considered to be honest and a man of his word.

Sam and John often helped each other with their farm work. One day, they had planned to plow a large field and had asked Cletus to help them. He claimed to have other things to do back at the farm and so refused to help them. They really hadn't expected him to help. He would always do anything possible to get out of work.

Later in the day, Sam and John stopped for a drink of water from the spring located at the end of the field near the country lane. They observed Cletus, riding a mule, going past them headed toward town.

"Where are you going?" John angrily yelled at Cletus, "Why don't you stop and tell us a big lie?"

"I don't have time." Cletus answered. "Dad just dropped dead."

After making this statement, he kicked his mule in the side and galloped down the lane toward town. John panicked. He and Sam unhooked the mules from the plow and almost killed them galloping the mile back to John's home. As they approached the farm house, they saw old man Keaton sitting on the porch rocking in his chair. There wasn't anything wrong with him except old age. He was ninety. On hot days he would sit in the shade and nap.

John was so angry with his brother Cletus, that he got his gun and started for town to to kill "that lying no good man."

Sam tried to talk him out of such a rash act, but John wouldn't listen. So Sam rode into town with John to calm him down before they reached town, which was about five miles away. On the way into town John kept saying that he couldn't believe that his brother would be so lazy and would tell such a lie about his father.

"He won't tell any more lies when I get through with him!" John swore.

When they entered town, there was Cletus sitting in the shade in front of the general store drinking a root beer. John and Sam got off their mules and tied them along side Cletus' mule, and then approached Cletus.

"What brings you to town?" Cletus said when he saw them." I thought you boys were plowing."

"John angrily replied, "I'm going to show you why I came to town," and then he pulled his pistol from his belt. Sam grabbed his arm and held it.

Cletus became very scared and said "What's the idea? What have I done to cause you to want to shoot me? I know I'm a little lazy, but you don't shoot people for being lazy."

"I'm not going to shoot you for being lazy," said John, "but for the big lie that you told me about pa."

"You told me to tell you a big lie," Cletus replied "and I sure did." This was too much. Both John and Sam broke into laughter. It was true. John had indeed told Cletus to stop and tell them a big lie.

Cletus maintained his reputation of being lazy and a liar throughout life, but he made a sincere effort to never tell his brother a lie again.

The Train Ride

It was in 1915 that Sam had an experience that would live with him all of his life. It was an incident that he could never forget, an incident of horror. He was 32 years old and well known in the Cherokee area. He was successful in his farming, active in local government and in the Methodist Church.

A Doctor Caldwell approached him with a problem. He had a patient who had contacted rabies from a fox bite and as a doctor he had done all he could for the unfortunate man. Any hope for a recovery for the affected man would be with doctors at the Memphis Memorial Hospital in Tennessee. He wanted to know if Sam would escort the man on the train to the hospital. Sam agreed because no one else would.

The unfortunate man was shackled to the train seat because he was irrational at times. He was moaning and groaning as they traveled toward Tennessee. He kept crying for water, and every time that Sam offered him a drink, he

154

would scream and throw the water away. He started foaming from the mouth and Sam and the other passengers became afraid that they, too, might contract that dreaded disease.

The victim would have fits and even at times would attempt to gnaw his wrists where the handcuffs were attached. He kept begging for water and repeating the incident of becoming crazier when he attempted to drink the water.

Sam was relieved when the train arrived in Memphis and was met by medical people from the hospital. The victim died the next day because there wasn't any hope for anyone who contacted rabies in those days. This incident was the worst experienced Sam was ever involved in. It was horrible to watch a person affected by such a terrible disease and not being able to help him.

Sam's Big Fight

Sam was a generous and kind person. He usually was friendly with everyone he had dealings with. Of course, like most people, he was prideful.

Anyone raised in the South during that period was necessarily involved with the racial situation, that is, segregation. There were a lot of black people living in that area of Alabama. Most of them earned their living by share-farming or doing farm work. Almost everyone was poor, including whites. Most however, had plenty to eat because they were able to raise their own food. Most had a milk cow, several hogs, chickens and always a large garden. The white people were somewhat better off than the average black person. Segregation was a fact of life and accepted as the way things were.

Sam worked as a manager for a large land owner

whose family had accumulated large tracts of land from the Reconstruction days after the Civil War. This land was broken into 40-acre tracts and share cropped. Sam's job was to manage the entire farm operation and collect the rent due the landowner at the end of each year.

A man, who farmed one of the forty-acre tracts, kept delaying his payment to Sam due for the year's sharecropping. He would always avoid Sam and told others he would not pay this year's rent because his crop was bad.

One day Sam was in Cherokee making some purchases at the general store, and he happened to meet the black sharecropper. Again, Sam asked him for the monies due for last year's rent. The man started giving Sam a lot of back talk, telling him he didn't think he would pay this year. This exchange was witnessed by several black and white customers in the store. Neither Sam nor the other man would back down.

One word led to another, and the man hit Sam in the chest. After exchanging several blows, Sam hit him in the chin and the blow caused the man to bite his tongue almost in half. The man started bleeding badly and almost bled to death before the doctor could stop the bleeding.

The man that Sam had struck in the mouth lingered between life and death for several days. He was relieved when the man recovered. Thereafter, when Sam requested the rent each year, this particular sharecropper was the first to pay. The man may not have liked Sam, but he did respect him.

Chapter 35
The Bad Decision

Milton was always a restless boy, but at the age of fifteen, he finally reached the Ninth Grade. He was attending Cherokee Vocational High School. After he had read all the "interesting" books in the school library, he became bored with school and with riding the bus 17 miles one way each day. After a while, he began attending only those classes that interested him, which were precious few. Since his mother and grandfather both worked, they were not aware of Milton decision.

During the second half of the school year, Milton was attending only physical education, social studies, and, occasionally, math. After the last of these classes, he would hitchhike to his favorite spot—Bear Creek.

At the creek, Milton had a small, home-made boat that wouldn't have passed anyone's safety standards anywhere in the world. Only the old coffee can he used for bailing kept him from sinking. He used that boat to fish—and to run fish traps—and to trap muskrats. It was also his transportation to the various "hot spots" along the creek. Milton would often come home from "school" with fish or some type of game—a rabbit or, perhaps, a muskrat. Neighbors would marvel at how Milton could be such an accomplished outdoorsman while attending school. When report-card time arrived, Milton did his mother "a favor" by simply signing her name for her. The forgery took some doing, but his imitation cleared his homeroom teacher.

And, even to Milton's surprise, he seemed always to pass, if just barely. But at end of the Ninth Grade Milton decided to quit school and devote full time to being an outdoorsman. More than anything, his decision was influenced by the many books of adventure he had read. He was truly motivated to do something different. He didn't want to grow up only to do the same things that everyone else did. For some reason, Milton had got it into his head that an education would make him nothing more than average, rather than raising him considerably above average, which was the purpose of education. In short, he once again was failing to apply himself.

At the end of the Ninth Grade, and with 82 days of unexcused absences behind him, Milton quit school. His mother strongly advised him against leaving school, but she had quit herself after finishing the Eighth Grade so it was difficult for her arguments to carry much weight. It bothered Milton to go against his mother's wishes, but, to him, school had become simply a burden: no one had ever sat him down and fully explained the advantages, not only of completing his education, but completing it well. After all, most of the adults Milton knew had not gone beyond the Seventh or Eighth Grade, and they were able to earn a living and seemed to be enjoying life, though he had to admit that some of them were sure narrow-minded.

With school now behind him and with a part-time job loading grocery trucks two hours each evening, Milton had money and plenty of time to hunt and fish. He was paid twelve dollars a week, which in 1947 wasn't bad money for a part-time job when you consider that movies only cost a quarter.

Before Milton had dropped out of school, he had joined the National Guard as a machine gunner, which was really fun for a 15-year-old. The half-track that the guns were mounted on was almost like a tank. Milton had never really considered that the day might come when all this would be something more than "child's play." The National Guard commander knew that Milton was only 15, but this was immediately after World War II, and no one wanted to be in the service. So, in desperation, the commander had accepted Milton as a "seventeen-year-old" to fill his quota in the Anti-Aircraft Company. Milton spend about a year in the guard. When he finally left, it was to join the Army Air Force, and that is another story for another time.

Chapter 36
Milton Joins the Marines

When he was sixteen, Milton decided that he wanted to a United States Marine. He had seen several movies about the war, and had talked with many of the returning servicemen. The movies and the stories of the young veterans convinced Milton that he was cut out to be a Marine.

Milton just knew he would make a good Marine: he was 5'9", weighed 120 pounds and had been toughened by both his outdoor and farm activities. But he thought it would be nice if he didn't have to go in alone, so he convinced five of his friends to join up with him and have the opportunity to become heroes.

There was one small problem, however. Milton was only 16, and his friends 17 and 18. Milton resolved that problem but resorting to a much-practiced trick: he forged his mother's name on his enlistment form. He returned the form to the recruiter and was given a date and time to depart for the United States Marines!

Milton spent much of the two weeks before he was due to depart just daydreaming. He imagined himself as a returning hero with wounds and medals—that is, few wounds and many medals. After all, it was his dream. The small town of Tuscumbia would surely have a parade in his honor.

But the time for dreaming finally passed, and the day of his departure arrived. His mother and grandparents gave him a tearful farewell, but his younger sister, Freida, didn't seemed much impressed. She hardly shed a tear and even seemed to be glad to see him leaving. Perhaps, she was thinking how nice it would be without Milton around to dominate her; her life would be much less of a hassle.

Milton caught a ride with his former boss at the rolling store warehouse and was dropped off at the bus station. He was carrying an old metal suitcase. He was to meet his friends and wait for the Marine recruiter to bring their tickets and orders.

The bus arrived before the recruiter, so the boys boarded the bus to wait. They were bragging about what heroic deeds they would perform with the Marines. Some were looking forward to all the pretty girls that the colorful uniform would attract. And Milton was just as boastful—which is to say, proud—as the others.

The recruiter soon arrived in his crisp Marine dress uniform, looking very military and stern. His first words were harsh and to the point: "Milton, get off the bus. I checked all your ages at the health department, and you're only sixteen. You shouldn't have lied to me."

It was a very depressed Milton that hitched a ride home where he told his family that he had decided not to join the Marines after all. They all were glad that he'd returned—even his sister. Milton was overwhelmed by the love of his family, but a part of him was sad that he wouldn't be a Marine hero.

When Milton turned seventeen, he did enter the service, but chose to join the Navy. When his Marine friends returned on leave and told him how tough boot-camp had been, Milton figured it was an experience that he could do without.

On the day he was to enlist with the Navy, Milton rode the bus to the Florence Courthouse, where the recruiting office was located. He walked to the second-floor office only to find himself in a long line outside the Navy recruitment center. He began to grow impatient; he disliked waiting in lines for anything. He glanced down the hall and saw the words "Army and Army Air Force" posted to the right of the door. The door was open, and two uniformed men stood in the doorway. When they saw Milton looking their way, they motioned for him to come to their office.

One of the sergeants asked Milton if he wanted to join the Army Air Corps. Milton answered that he had planned to join the Navy. They asked if he was a strong swimmer, and Milton had to admit that he was not. The sergeant told Milton the obvious: that ships were often sunk, and sailors had to be strong swimmers to survive in shark-infested waters until they could be picked up. He then asked Milton if he knew James Lewey from Tuscumbia. Milton knew, as everyone in Tuscumbia did, that James Lewey's ship had been sunk in a naval battle in the Pacific, and James had been in the water all night with sharks around him. The story—as it had the first time he heard it—caused Milton to shudder: it was bad enough being in a boat at night on Bear Creek in snake-infested waters. Suddenly, the Navy, like the Marines, would have to make do without Milton.

He asked the recruiter to tell him about the Army Air Corps, and the recruiter was more than happy to oblige. Before he knew it, Milton had signed the papers and set a date for his departure. It was April 4, 1949. Milton had been seventeen for nineteen days. He felt good about his decision;

after all, he would be able to fly a lot farther than he could swim. He would be paid seventy-five dollars a month with free meals and place to sleep. For Milton, this deal was too good to believe. The only thing that bothered Milton was that one of the sergeants winked at the other when they thought he wasn't looking. They seemed amused about something, and Milton wondered what it was....

There are many more Milton stories, enough to fill another book. Now, that's an idea....THE END FOR NOW.

JMH